The Mystery of the Transfiguration

The Mystery of Christmas: A Commentary on the Magnificat, Gloria and Nunc Dimittis

The Mystery of Easter, translated by Alan Neame

The Mystery of God's Word, translated by Alan Neame

The Mystery of Pentecost, translated by Glen S. Davis

Obedience: The Authority of the Word, translated by Frances Lonergan Villa

The Power of the Cross

Poverty, translated by Charles Serignat

Remember Jesus Christ: Responding to the Challenges of Faith in Our Time, translated by Marsha Daigle-Williamson, PH.D.

Sober Intoxication of the Spirit: Filled With the Fullness of God, translated by Marsha Daigle-Williamson, PH.D.

St. Francis and the Cross: Reflections on Suffering, Weakness, and Joy, with Carlo Maria Martini

This Is My Body: Eucharistic Reflections Inspired by Adoro Te Devote *and* Ave Verum

Virginity: A Positive Approach to Celibacy for the Sake of the Kingdom of Heaven, translated by Charles Serignat

THE MYSTERY
—— *of the* ——
TRANSFIGURATION

RANIERO CANTALAMESSA, O.F.M. CAP.

Translated by Marsha Daigle-Williamson, PH.D.

PUBLISHED BY ST. ANTHONY MESSENGER PRESS
CINCINNATI, OHIO

The Mystery of the Transfiguration was published originally as *Il Mistero della Transfigurazione,* copyright ©1999 by Ancora Editrice, Italy.

Scripture passages have been taken from the *New Revised Standard Version Bible,* copyright ©1989 by the Division of Christian Education of the National Council of the Churches of Christ in the U.S.A., and used by permission. All rights reserved.

(Notes: The editors of this volume have made minor changes in capitalization to some of the Scripture quotations herein. Please consult the original source for proper capitalization.)

Cover design and image by Candle Light Studios
Interior design by Jennifer Tibbits

LIBRARY OF CONGRESS CATALOGING-IN-PUBLICATION DATA

Cantalamessa, Raniero.
 [Mistero della Transfigurazione. English]
 The mystery of the transfiguration / Raniero Cantalamessa ; translated by Marsha Daigle-Williamson,.
     p. cm.
 Includes bibliographical references and index.
 ISBN 978-0-86716-802-0 (pbk. : alk. paper) 1. Jesus Christ—Transfiguration. I. Title.

BT410.C3613 2008
232.9 56—dc22

                                    2007040914

ISBN: 978-0-86716-802-0

Published by Servant Books, an imprint of St. Anthony Messenger Press
28 W. Liberty St.
Cincinnati, OH 45202
www.ServantBooks.org

Printed in the United States of America

Printed on acid-free paper

08 09 10 11 12 5 4 3 2 1

CONTENTS

This volume completes a series of meditations on the "the mystery of Christ in the life of the Church." It follows meditations on the mysteries of the birth of Christ, his baptism, his preaching, the paschal mystery and Pentecost.

The book's theme is Christ's Transfiguration, viewed from a particular angle: It does not simply recount the Gospel event but approaches the Transfiguration insofar as it constitutes a mystery in the life of Christ. The phrase "mystery in the life of Christ," according to traditional Latin spirituality, means a historical event in Christ's life that is full of salvific significance, that is, that has an exemplary and causative value for the members of his body, the Church.

After an introductory chapter on the approach and the goal of our journey, there are six chapters, each of which is conceived as a morning ascent of Mount Tabor to spend time in contemplation of Christ.

First we will ascend with the three apostles who were physically present on the "holy mountain," following the Gospel account step by step. Then we will ascend in the company of Paul and John, the greatest probers of the mystery of Christ, and finally we will ascend in the company of the great teachers of antiquity who most contributed to the image of Christ in dogma, liturgy and the piety of the Church up to the present day. We will draw from them the inspiration to outline a picture of Christ for people in the third millennium.

The essential goal of this book is to encourage contemplation of Christ, to enkindle in us a desire for it and to nourish it with the powerful revelation of the Bible and some of the most profound insights of the Fathers. These meditations, originally delivered to the papal household in the year of preparation for the Jubilee dedicated to Christ, attempt to gather the salient characteristics of the Savior transmitted to us through Tradition to enhance the image of Christ that we could have in the third millennium.

CHAPTER I

EYEWITNESSES OF HIS MAJESTY

A Mystagogical Approach to the Transfiguration

THE TRANSFIGURATION IN THE EAST AND WEST

There are four Gospel passages that have a special status in Lent and can be used in all three liturgical cycles: the Transfiguration, Jesus' encounter with the Samaritan woman, the healing of the man born blind and the resurrection of Lazarus. Among these events, only the Transfiguration is called a mystery in the life of Christ. Why? Because in all the other cases, *Jesus does something:* He promises living water, heals a blind man, raises a dead man. In other words, he is giving a teaching or performing a miracle. In the Transfiguration *something is happening to Jesus.* In this case, he is not only the performer of the miraculous action but also its recipient. In the Transfiguration, as in his birth, his baptism and later his death and resurrection, not only does he accomplish something, but something is also operating in him that directs the course of his life and clarifies the meaning of his mission.

The Transfiguration, like all the mysteries of Christ's life, has been actualized at a communal level, in the Church's liturgy. A brief observation in this regard will illuminate the goals of our subsequent reflection. In the East the Transfiguration became a feast from the eighth century on, and in some regions a foremost feast. In the West the feast of the Transfiguration on August 6 was introduced only in 1457 by Pope Callistus III for a specific purpose: in gratitude for the victory over the Turks in Belgrade the previous year. Even from the time of Saint Leo the Great in the fifth century, the Gospel passage for the second Sunday in Lent chosen by the Latins is the Transfiguration.

This fact has profoundly influenced the way this Gospel event has been understood in the West. The Transfiguration has always been viewed above all in its *pedagogical,* or *teaching,* dimension. According to Saint Leo the Great, Jesus

> used the Transfiguration chiefly that the scandal of the Cross would be lifted from the hearts of the disciples, and that the humility of his voluntary suffering would not upset the faith of those to whom the perfection of his hidden dignity had been revealed.[1]

The Transfiguration has never entered into Latin spirituality as a separate mystery, endowed with its own significance, but only in connection to Easter, as a counterbalance to the scandal of the Passion and as a promise of the Resurrection. Before we set out on a difficult path, we first need to know our destination, just as the archer determines his target before he shoots the arrow, and according to Saint Thomas Aquinas the Transfiguration belongs in this category.[2]

The situation in Orthodox spirituality is quite different. In that tradition the Transfiguration has been the object of a special feast from the very beginning and is seen as a mystery that has meaning in itself and not just in relation to Easter. Anastasius of Sinai wrote that on Tabor

> the mystery of the crucifixion was announced, the beauty of the kingdom was revealed, and Christ's coming in glory was manifested.... It prefigured our future image and our configuration in Christ.... The feast today reveals the other Sinai that is even more precious than the first.[3]

Here the *mystagogical* aspect of the feast prevails over its pedagogical aspect, which is also present. For Leo the Great as well, "the hope of the holy church was made firm" in the Transfiguration.[4] However, in the West it is seen as a teaching that God gave to the Church on that occasion. The presence of Moses and Elijah, for example, is "instruction" that is given "to strengthen the apostles and advance them to all knowledge."[5]

For the Eastern Church Jesus is less the master who imparts teaching on this occasion than he is the Son of God who reveals himself to his disciples. The Transfiguration is a theophany, or better, a "Christophany." Not only is it a mystery that has a meaning in its own right, but it is also, in a certain sense, the core mystery that unites all the other mysteries, a mountain peak that gives a bird's-eye view of both slopes of the story of salvation, that is, the Old and New Testaments. The Transfiguration *fulfills the past:* the Creation (with the manifestation of the true image of God), Sinai, the law and the prophets; it also *anticipates the future:* the glory of the Resurrection, the Second Coming and the final glory of the righteous.

If there is a moment in which Christ appears as "the center of all time," it is the Transfiguration. Jesus is not only the center "of all time" but also of "all worlds," the divine and the human worlds. The Jesus of the icons who is standing at the summit of the mount—on the highest peak of the rock where earth ends and the sky begins—is an eloquent affirmation of the dogma from the Council of Chalcedon that Jesus Christ is at the same time "truly God and truly man,"[6] God and man united in one and the same person. The Transfiguration offers a wholly evangelical way of preaching Christocentrism.

It is true that all of this will be definitively recapitulated in the paschal mystery of the death and resurrection of Christ, but it is manifested beforehand in the Transfiguration as a kind of prophetic sign. Just as Jesus anticipates his death and reveals its meaning through the breaking of the bread and the offering of the cup when instituting the Eucharist, so too—although not in a sacramental sense—he prefigures and anticipates in the Transfiguration the glorification that will occur in his resurrection. On par with certain symbolic acts by prophets in the Old Testament, the Transfiguration is "a creative prefiguration of the future which would be speedily and inevitably realized."[7] In other words, the glorification of Christ is not only prefigured but has already begun.

Through Contemplation We Are Transfigured

In order for an event in Jesus' life to be a mystery, it is not enough, however, that "something is accomplished in Christ." The event must also have a salvific significance for his whole body in that it is a pattern and an effective cause for the members of the Church. According to Saint Augustine this is what distinguishes a simple "anniversary" from a celebration that is "in the category of mystery" *(in sacramento)*. The only thing required for an anniversary celebration is the annual return of the date on which an event occurred. For a celebration in the category of mystery, however, the impact that such an event has today and the part we play in it are very significant.[8] On the Feast of the Transfiguration, the Church celebrates not only Christ's transfiguration but her own as well.

What transfiguration do I mean? Above all, the eschatological transfiguration that will happen at the end of time, when the Lord Jesus, as the apostle Paul says, "will transform the body of our humiliation so that it may be conformed to the body of his glory" (Philippians 3:21). According to Proclus of Constantinople, "Christ was transfigured to show us the future transfiguration of our nature and his second coming."[9] This concept is also present in the West. The Transfiguration, writes Saint Leo the Great, occurred "so that it [the Church] might know with what sort of exchange the whole body of Christ was to be given, and that the members might promise to themselves a sharing in the honor of the one who had shone as their Head."[10]

Even in antiquity there were some who saw not only our final transformation but also that of the whole cosmos prefigured in the Transfiguration. On Tabor, says Anastasius of Sinai, Christ "transfigured all of creation into his image and recreated it in an even more sublime way."[11] The person who gave this concept a modern expression was Pierre Teilhard de Chardin. For him the Transfiguration was "the most beautiful mystery of Christianity," the feast that expressed precisely all that he believed in and hoped for, that is, a universe that was transfigured and rendered "Christlike," with divinity shining through all of creation in the end, just as on Tabor it shone through the flesh of Christ in an analogous, but not identical, manner.[12]

However, the Transfiguration of Christ concerns his mystical body not only in the next life but in this life as well. Saint Paul twice uses the verb meaning "*to be transfigured*" (in Greek "*to be transfigured*" and "*to be transformed*" are the same word) in reference to Christians, and in both texts they indicate something that happens here and now: "*Be transformed* by the renewing of your minds" (Romans 12:2, emphasis added). In the second text Paul also explains how that will happen: "And all of us, with unveiled faces, seeing the glory of the Lord as though reflected in a mirror, are being *transformed* into the same image from one degree of glory to another; for this comes from the Lord, the Spirit" (2 Corinthians 3:18, emphasis added).

It is through contemplation that we can enter into the mystery of the Transfiguration here and now, make it ours and participate in it. The phrase that is translated as "reflected in a mirror" can have two meanings. The first, used by the ancients, means "to contemplate as in a mirror." The second meaning, more in use today, is "to reflect as in a mirror." In the first case, Christ is the mirror in which we contemplate his divine glory; in the second case, we are the mirror that, as we gaze on Christ, reflects his divine glory.

The older interpretation was sometimes criticized because people thought it put Christ on the same level as the rest of creation, which was also described as a mirror (see 1 Corinthians 13:12), but there is nothing that obliges us to think that the apostle Paul used the word *mirror* with the same meaning in both texts. In a similar example, a human being is the image of God, but that does not prevent the apostle from describing Christ as the "image of God" (see Colossians 1:15) in a different and more profound sense. The nuances of both meanings of "reflected in a mirror" can coexist, as they do in a modern authorized translation of the Bible that says we can understand the expression to mean "we contemplate and reflect" or, in other words, "we reflect that which we contemplate."[13]

According to the apostle, even more must be said. A person not only *reflects* what is contemplated but *becomes* what is contemplated. While contemplating we become transformed into the image we contemplate. This is a concept whose profound truth we are perhaps better able to grasp today. If at one time, at the beginning of scientific materialism, it was said that "a person is what he or she eats," now, in a culture wholly dominated by images and visual communication, it can be said that "a person is what he or she looks at." An image has the power to penetrate not only the body but even the soul through the imagination. "The eye is the lamp of the body" (Matthew 6:22), but it is also the doorway to the soul.

Therefore, the apostle says that in contemplating Christ we become like him, we conform ourselves to him. We are allowed access to his world, his purposes, his sentiments, so that we can imprint them on ourselves; so that we can substitute his thoughts, his purposes and his sentiments for ours; so that we can make ourselves like him. There is a curious parallel between contemplation and photography. The verb "to photograph" occurred for the first time with a Byzantine author of the twelfth century, precisely to indicate what transpires when the soul contemplates Christ: "[L]et us guard the heart with all diligence from thoughts that obscure the soul's mirror; for in that mirror Jesus Christ, the wisdom and power of God the Father (cf. 1 Cor

1:24), is typified and luminously reflected *(photeinographein)*."[14] But haven't we already discovered this at our own expense? Certain images have the power to engrave themselves on our minds and to stay with us like graffiti on cement walls.

THE ASCENT OF MOUNT TABOR

Tabor initiates and continues to issue the strongest call to the transforming contemplation of Christ. This is the mystery par excellence for the contemplation of Jesus. On the "holy mountain," as Saint Peter calls it, the apostles were *epoptai*: contemplators, spectators, eyewitnesses of the majesty of Jesus (see 2 Peter 1:16–18). In the other mysteries of Christ's life, sacramental or liturgical actualization predominates; in the Transfiguration the channel of contemplation predominates. There is, in fact, no actual sacrament to celebrate the Transfiguration, as there is for the baptism of Christ and for his death and resurrection.

I want not merely to offer a *reflection* on the theme of the contemplation of Christ but also—insofar as possible in a book—to offer an *experience* of contemplation. I would like to go beyond the idea to "the reality itself." I have therefore conceived of the meditations in this book as several morning-prayer ascents to Mount Tabor for us to spend a half an hour "looking to Jesus the pioneer and perfecter of our faith" (Hebrews 12:2) and to return fortified for our daily tasks.

Paul VI, who loved the mystery of the Transfiguration very much, wrote in a notation during a personal retreat,

To know Christ, one must believe in him. The attack of incomplete or false exegesis, habitual verbal formulas, the weariness inflicted on one's mind by our times, and so many other perverted or depressing thoughts weaken us and sometimes eclipse, even for faithful followers, the transfigured knowledge of Jesus, the marvel, the joy, the progressive discovery of his human-divine reality. Thus, what is needed, while the twilight of this present life lasts, is that our contemplation of Jesus Christ be continually reawakened.[15]

In a time dominated by an intense search for "objective," historical and philological certainty about Jesus, the Church has an imperative need to rediscover some of this "transfigured knowledge" of Christ that was once so alive in a way that does not deny but transcends "scientific" knowledge.

Gospel events run the risk of being "dissected," of being reduced to mere facts and thus losing the life that flows in them. The Transfiguration, viewed this way, is remembered and celebrated for its external trappings, according to the "letter" of the event, but the hearts that beat behind the actions and the words are no longer perceived. The aim of contemplation is precisely to go beyond the letter and to relive the event with the feelings and the mindsets of the participants: Jesus, the apostles and the heavenly Father himself when he proclaimed, "This is my Son, the Beloved" (Matthew 17:5; Mark 9:7). Icon painters, representing Moses and Elijah leaning toward Jesus liked curved bows, invite us to identify ourselves with them and to make their attitude of unbounded adoration our own. All of this can happen when the contemplation of the Transfiguration occurs within that same "bright cloud" (Matthew 17:5) in which the event transpired, that is, "in the Holy Spirit."

Our contemplation will thus not be purely subjective, that is, dependent only on our current capacity. Rather, we will strive to participate in the important contemplation of Christ begun in the Scripture and followed uninterruptedly in Tradition. From that vantage point there is a profound affinity between a meditation on the Transfiguration and an icon of the Transfiguration.

We know the importance of the icon of the Transfiguration in the East. Icon painters used to begin their artistic endeavors with that subject. This icon is the mother of all icons in the sense that the same light that shone forth on Tabor should be reflected in every icon. Every icon of Christ should allow us to glimpse the invisible through the visible, just as the divinity of Christ shone through the veil of his flesh on Tabor.

But how does the artist go about depicting the Transfiguration? He does not set out to invent anything; he does not aspire to be original, as a secular artist would. Instead, he receives a fixed pattern from tradition and tries to bring it to life again; he does not merely "make a copy," he "makes it anew." If need be he will vary a color or the placement of a particular element; more often he will reduce the component parts and simplify, always aiming at the essential.

A mystagogical meditation like this one does the same thing. It does not try to discover new things about the Transfiguration that were never said before. It tries instead to gather together the best that the Holy Spirit has revealed about it in the past, bringing to life that heritage in language that is tailored to modern-day people and, if possible, to add some new insight, however small, since the mysteries of Christ, like his words, are "spirit and life" (see John 6:63) and never cease revealing all of their hidden riches.

THE TRANSFIGURATION: A "HISTORICAL" EVENT

I said that for our contemplation of Christ we would lean on those who have gone before us in faith. The departure point will naturally be the three apostles who contemplated the event itself, or more precisely, the three evangelists who narrate the story, the first of whom, Mark, was able to benefit from the firsthand testimony of Peter.

The Gospel accounts of the Transfiguration already constitute, in their own way, a contemplation of the mystery, that is, an attempt to plumb the depth of its meaning. That is clearly demonstrated by the different emphases present in each of them. One could object, "If we do that, don't we risk shifting from the solid ground of the event to the developing ground of theological interpretations that came after Easter?" No, because these theological interpretations are also part of the historical nucleus of the event, if by "historical" event we mean the event plus its significance and not merely the bare, crude facts that are chronicled. An infinite number of events have actually transpired that, nevertheless, are not "historical" because they have left no trace in history: They have neither generated interest nor birthed anything new. According to C.H. Dodd, "an historical 'event' is an occurrence *plus* the interest and meaning which the occurrence possessed for the persons involved in it, and by which the record is determined."[16]

In that sense the Transfiguration, as narrated in the Gospels, is a legitimate historical event. A comparison with the conversion of Saint Paul can shed light here. Let us suppose someone, even Paul himself, had described in great detail what had happened on the road to Damascus immediately after the event. Then let us think about how Paul understands the event of conversion and presents it much later, when he highlights certain aspects of it in the Letter to the Galatians and elsewhere (see Galatians 1:17; Acts 26:12–18). Let us also think about the reverberations that such an event had in the Acts of the Apostles and in all the early Church. Which of the two presentations would do more justice to the event and hold more historical truth? Many difficulties in scriptural interpretation arise from ignorance about spiritual phenomena and their particular characteristics.

Should we not use a similar judgment when we speak of the historicity of the Gospel accounts of the Transfiguration? On this point what a famous exegete recently wrote at the end of his commentary on the Transfiguration seems very balanced and accurate to me:

> The most obvious interpretation for an event in Jesus' life is that it is to be understood and expressed in its unique relevance by reference to the variety of different Old Testament and apocalyptic conceptions.... The account makes us think of a real event that transpired in Jesus rather than of a subjective vision that three disciples, or one of them, had.[17]

In the case of Tabor, the meanings brought to light by the evangelists with recourse to the "variety of Old Testament conceptions" do not, in the strict sense, "add" anything new or extraneous to the event but rather "extract" and highlight portions of its inexhaustible content. We often see a moment of revelation in the lives of the saints and other great men and women of faith, a profound and definitive contact with the divine, whose import is manifested only little by little as we see its fulfillment in the course of their lives. To deny the historical nature and the supernatural objective character of the Transfiguration as attested by the

Gospels would mean that it is impossible to believe about Christ what is seen in the lives of the saints (in different ways, of course, and with different meanings). The history of the saints offers us well-documented cases of their authentic transfigurations, as in the case of Saint Seraphim of Sarov recounted by his disciple, Motovilov.[18]

JESUS IS TRANSFIGURED IN THE SCRIPTURES

The Synoptic accounts of the Transfiguration are themselves a Tabor for us to ascend—the cloud in which to enter and the veil that must be drawn aside to allow us to contemplate Christ in this mystery. I will not comment separately on each of the three accounts (Matthew 17:1–9; Mark 9:2–9; Luke 9:28–36) but will look at them together as a whole. In fact, for the sake of contemplation, there is no need to point out the differences and uniqueness of each one; the focus rather is on the unity that exists in all three accounts. (To dwell on the minutiae of the text, while we are in an attitude of contemplation, would be as if the apostles, right in the middle of the Transfiguration on Tabor, had begun discussing what material Elijah's sandals were made of!)

One can contemplate the Transfiguration either through the icon or through the words of the Gospels or, even better, through both methods at once. Paraphrasing what Augustine said about word and sacrament, we can say that an icon is a word that is made visible, while the word is an image that is heard.

Unlike what happens with all other icons, the power in the Transfiguration icon does not reside in Christ's gaze—his gaze is hardly noted in the reduced space that he occupies in the scene. Its power instead comes from the whole, and especially from his garments. In fact, that "whiteness" itself should demonstrate the mystery of divine light radiating from within Christ. According to Origen, the words of the Gospel are also, in their own way, the garments of Christ:

> When…you see any one not only with a thorough understanding of the theology concerning Jesus, but also making clear every expression of the Gospels, do not hesitate to say that to Him [sic] the garments of Jesus have become white as light.[19]

Jesus is still transfigured today in the Scripture, and in order to make his garments white, that is, to make his words clear and understandable, intelligence is not enough. No launderer on earth, says the evangelist Mark, would have been able to make clothes as white as those of Jesus on Tabor (see Mark 9:3). No scholarly reading in and of itself, then, can illuminate the mystery contained in Scripture—in this case, in the Transfiguration. Only the Holy Spirit can do that. The Gospel account that we are preparing to contemplate can become a burning bush for us through which God reveals his face in a definitive way, or it can remain an arid account that means nothing—exactly as barren and bleak as Tabor would have seemed the day before and the day after the memorable event.

CHAPTER 2

TRANSFIGURED BEFORE THEM

On Tabor With the Three Apostles

"JESUS TOOK WITH HIM PETER AND JAMES AND JOHN"

Let us begin the first ascent of our spiritual Tabor right now. Six days after receiving Peter's profession of faith and announcing his Passion in Caesarea Philippi (see Mark 8:27—9:1), Jesus took Peter, James and John with him and went "up a high mountain apart, by themselves" (Mark 9:2). Through these three descriptors ("high," "apart," "by themselves"), the event is detached from the natural realm and the rhythm of ordinary life and moves into a different dimension—one of solitude, silence and distance from everything.

The first stanza of the poem "The Ascent of Mount Carmel" by Saint John of the Cross helps put us in the frame of mind of someone who leaves everything behind and, while it is still the middle of the night, leaves the house on tiptoe, so as not to be detained, to follow the call of the beloved:

> On a dark night,
>
> Kindled in love with yearnings—oh, happy chance!—
>
> I went forth without being observed
>
> My house being now at rest.[1]

The "house" we must leave consists of the material things and preoccupations from which we need to free ourselves. Each of us will easily know what that means. There must be a detachment, a break, just like the one Jacob made when he was about to wrestle with God. He sent his wives, his concubines, his herds and everything else across the river Jabbok, remaining alone on the other side (see Genesis 32:23–24).

Jesus, the Gospel says, "was transfigured before them" (Matthew 17:2). He was not transfigured before all the people indiscriminately in the midst of a bustling crowd but only before those who had left below relatives, friends, work—everything— and had accepted his invitation to come aside with him. These are the ones who can say with the psalmist, "Your face, LORD, do I seek. Do not hide your face from me" (Psalm 27:8–9), or "My heart is ready, O God, my heart is ready" (Psalm 57:7).[2]

Let us read as we proceed: "His face shone like the sun, and his clothes became dazzling white" (Matthew 17:2). What can be clearly deduced from the text is that the light does not envelop Jesus from without, but comes forth from within him. His face is not simply "illuminated" but "shines forth." The same is true for his clothes: They become "dazzling white." This highlights the essential difference between the Transfiguration and similar theophanies in the Old Testament. Jesus is shining with his own—not reflected—light; his face reflects not merely the glory of God, as was the case with Moses' face (see 2 Corinthians 3:13), but also his own glory. More precisely, he is resplendent with his own glory, the very glory of God, because he is the radiance "of God's glory and the exact imprint of God's very being" (Hebrews 1:3).

This point also expresses the essence of what the Transfiguration means for our understanding of the person of Christ. Jesus is not part of the series of famous personages in the Old Testament who saw the glory of God and received a theophany, even if he would head that list. He stands apart. He does not see God but rather is seen as God. A new kind of theophany is inaugurated on Tabor, a "Christophany."

The Fathers expanded on this Gospel fact. Saint John Chrysostom asks, "What does it mean that 'he was transfigured'? It means that he revealed something about his divinity and showed them the God which dwelled in his flesh."[3] Saint John of Damascus specifies, "He was transfigured, not taking on something that he was not, but demonstrating to his disciples exactly who he was."[4]

"WHILE HE WAS PRAYING, HIS FACE SHONE LIKE THE SUN"

We cannot, however, reduce the Transfiguration to this objective, revelatory aspect that would benefit others but not Jesus himself. The Transfiguration, like the Resurrection later, is not primarily a subject for apologetics but a mysterious event. It is above all a gift that the Father gives to Jesus, a way of showing him his favor. On Tabor Jesus is not so much a master who imparts teachings or furnishes proofs of his divinity to his disciples as he is the Son who allows his friends to share a moment of intimacy between himself and the heavenly Father so that they can be witnesses to and participants in his glory.

Jesus is not "performing" a part before his disciples. Everything here is real, just as everything that will soon occur in front of these same three disciples at Gethsemane will be real and not merely pedagogical. On that day Jesus, in his humanity, went into ecstasy! That is perhaps the least inadequate way of describing what was happening in Jesus—a special ecstasy. Jesus, in fact, is the only person who does not need to "go out of himself" to enter into God. There is a kind of short circuit in him (if I can use that image) between divinity and humanity. The "insulation," which was his human flesh, is "fused" with divinity and itself becomes light and energy.

He was happy. The Transfiguration is a mystery of divine happiness. The whole stream of joy that flows between the Father and Son, which is the Holy Spirit himself, "overflowed" the vessel of Christ's humanity on this occasion.

How do we know this subjective aspect of the Transfiguration? Luke was deliberate in specifying one point: Jesus ascended the mountain "to pray," and it was "while he was praying" (Luke 9:29) that his countenance changed. The Transfiguration is a direct effect of Jesus' prayer. To whom was Jesus praying, and with whom was he conversing, if not the Father? The Gospels are unanimous that all of Jesus' prayers begin with the filial cry of "*Abba!*" and consist of open and loving conversation with the Father. Jesus came close to ecstasy one other time when he was praying—when he "rejoiced in the Holy Spirit and said, 'I thank you, Father'" (Luke 10:21).

What occurs in the Transfiguration is exactly what occurred at the baptism in the Jordan. There too it was Jesus' prayer that opened heaven and called down the Spirit: "When Jesus also had been baptized *and was praying*, the heaven was opened" (Luke 3:21, emphasis added).

Jesus did not climb Tabor that day to be transfigured. He was not thinking of that in the least. This was a surprise that the Father had in store for him. As we heard, he climbed to pray, to respond to a compelling call to conversation with the Father.

"*And while he was praying*, the appearance of his face changed" (Luke 9:29, emphasis added). This is not simply an insignificant addition by Luke; it is the key to understanding the whole event. And it is also what instantly brings the Transfiguration close to us, not just as a mystery to contemplate but also to imitate. If the aim of contemplating Christ, as Paul told us, is to be transformed and become like the one we contemplate, if we too are called to be transfigured, then prayer is the foremost path to achieve that.

In all the Gospels there is not one image or scene that is more compelling than that of Jesus praying to the Father—whether it is evening or night or early dawn when it is still dark, on a mountain or on the shore of a lake. This is a striking image that has the power to attract the mind and heart, to catalyze our thoughts and desires. It enthralls us.

The Gospels do not tell us the content of those long nights or hours of Jesus' prayer. But one thing is certain: A vortex was established between the place on earth where the Son of God was praying and heaven, a direct communication. These were the times when Jesus' words to Nathaniel had their fulfillment: "You will see heaven opened and the angels of God ascending and descending upon the Son of Man" (John 1:51). All the love and life of the Trinity passed through that vortex. And we were not absent from that place. "I will pray for you," Jesus tells his apostles. "I have prayed for you," he says to Peter (Luke 22:32), and he prays "on behalf of those who will believe in me through their [the apostles'] word" (John 17:20)—precisely for us, today's disciples.

There is a miniature from the eleventh century on Mount Athos in Greece that shows Jesus in prayer on the slope of a mountain. In front of and above him, we see the figure of the Father in a semicircle. Behind Jesus the apostles are exchanging silent glances, as if to say, "See how he prays!" Perhaps it was during a similar instance that they were impressed and asked Jesus, "Lord, teach us to pray" (Luke 11:1). We, too, before going any further, need to direct that same request to Jesus: "Lord, teach us to pray!"

"THERE APPEARED TO THEM MOSES AND ELIJAH"

The meaning of the Transfiguration that I have called "objective"—its significance for salvation history and for understanding the person of Christ—is especially revealed through the presence of Moses and Elijah. From early on they have been seen as representatives of the law and of the prophets, respectively. But perhaps they are here to recall the occasion when each of them had a revelation of God on Mount Sinai (see Exodus 19; 33—34; 1 Kings 9:9—13). The parallel between Sinai and Tabor is readily seen, so much so that when the church of Saint Catherine's monastery on the slope of Sinai opened in the sixth century, it is said that a mosaic depicting the scene of the Transfiguration appeared spontaneously in the vault of the apse, and this became the model for all the icons on the Transfiguration. An ancient Father explains the connection between the two mountains this way:

> Mount Tabor surpasses Sinai: on Sinai there was a flame of fire (Ex
> 3:2), but on Tabor the light of divinity (Mt 17:2); on Sinai a bush, on
> Tabor a cloud; on Sinai, Moses, the glorious servant, on Tabor, the
> very Lord of glory himself; on Sinai the figure, on Tabor the reality.
> No longer the law given through Moses, but grace and truth given
> through Jesus Christ (cf. Jn 1:17).[5]

Moses truly finds himself now before the "burning bush"; now
he hears the great "I AM" speak; his desire to "see the glory of
God" is satisfied (see Exodus 33:18–23). No longer does he contemplate only God's "back" as he lies hidden in the cleft of a rock;
the "hand" that protects Moses' eyes now is the flesh of Christ, in
which God has veiled himself.[6]

The commonalities and differences between Tabor and Sinai
will appear more clearly in the rest of the account, when the
Father's voice is heard. For now let us pause for an important
detail. Mark and Matthew simply say that Moses and Elijah "were
talking" with Jesus, but Luke specifies what they were talking
about: "his departure, which he was about to accomplish at
Jerusalem" (Luke 9:31).

Moses and Elijah are not instructing Jesus about the destiny
of his Passion because he had already announced it shortly
before to his disciples (see Luke 9:22, 44). Instead they serve as a
confirmation from heaven of Jesus' word. After the Resurrection,
Jesus, "beginning with Moses and all the prophets," explained to
the disciples at Emmaus how he "should suffer these things and
enter into his glory" (Luke 24: 26, 27). Something similar implicitly occurs here before those events take place.

The Passion is found at the very heart of the mystery of the
Transfiguration. The glory of Jesus cannot be separated, even for

one instant, from the cross. The Transfiguration is completely different from pagan apotheoses. It is the revelation of a new kind of glory and power that springs forth precisely from the renunciation of all power and glory. He "emptied himself.... He humbled himself and became obedient to the point of death.... *Therefore,* God also highly exalted him" (Philippians 2:7–9, emphasis added).

Luke implicitly completes the reference to the Passion, noting that "Peter and his companions were weighed down with sleep" (Luke 9:32). This very detail foreshadows what will happen at Gethsemane. It is worth pausing a moment with this picture of the three disciples, who are distracted and full of sleep at such a time, in order to open our own eyes and realize how many times we ourselves are those sleepy and distracted disciples. We were at the altar receiving the Eucharist; Jesus was present, not merely transfigured but transubstantiated in the bread and wine before us. Along with Moses and Elijah, hosts of angels were there without daring to "look upon" him, but we were distracted and our minds were wandering. Or perhaps someone was preaching the Word of God and our eyes were heavy with sleep, and we were barely able to stifle a yawn.

There is a saying from Saint Francis that often comes to mind when I also find myself in that state: "It is a great misery and a miserable weakness that when you have Him present with you in this way, you concern yourselves with anything else in this entire world."[7]

"Master, It Is Good (*kalon*) for Us to Be Here!"

The use of the word *kalon* in the context of the Transfiguration is not accidental. The Hebrew term can mean *beautiful* or *good;*

the Septuagint translated it as *beautiful*. At the end of the week of Creation, God saw that everything was "good" or "beautiful" (Genesis 1:4, 10, 12, 18, 21, 25). Now, with the manifestation of the new man, of the true and perfect image of God, the true beauty that was lost though sin reappears. The Transfiguration is also the most fitting mystery, with its exultation of light, to introduce us to the contemplation of beauty. This occurs especially in the spirituality that is linked to the art of icons.

According to a famous exegete,

> Her [Israel's] most intense encounter with beauty was in the religious sphere, in the contemplation of Jahweh's revelation and action; and because of this concentration of the experience of beauty upon the *credenda* ["the object of faith"], Israel occupies a special place in the history of aesthetics.[8]

It is especially in describing the apparition of God, the theophany, that the biblical authors developed an aesthetic sense. Such descriptions "contain what are probably the most intensified statements about beauty in the whole of the Old Testament."[9] Everything that has come in contact with God's presence is beautiful. Mount Zion is "the perfection of beauty" (see Psalm 50:2) precisely because it is God's dwelling place. Everything that is connected to God, even the feet of his messengers, becomes beautiful (see Isaiah 52:7).

It is not a surprise, therefore, that the new theophany on Tabor became for Christians the subject par excellence for aesthetic representation and the occasion for the celebration of beauty. According to Anastasius of Sinai, "Today on Tabor he renewed and transformed the image of earthly beauty into an image of heavenly beauty."[10]

We know from experience what kind of hold beauty has on people, especially since they are created in the image of God who is infinite beauty. Eastern culture was based in large part on this value. We can say that the quest for and the cult of beauty is the most novel and explicit characteristic of classical culture. Other cultures have placed more emphasis on power, as seen in their imposing buildings, or on the gruesome and the fantastic. What we are primarily heirs of in the West is a focus on beauty.

However, this beauty was often conceived as separate from the good and the sacred. It was no longer understood the way Plato defined it, as the "splendor of truth."[11] When it ends up as the exultation of physical forms, beauty is transformed into a dangerous idol and becomes, for the spiritual person who seeks to free himself or herself from material things, one of the most difficult obstacles to overcome, precisely because of its affinity to the good and the true.

We are familiar with Augustine's bitter lament:

> Late have I loved you, Beauty so ancient and so new,
> late have I loved you!
> Lo, you were within,
> but I outside, seeking there for you,
> and upon the shapely things you have made I rushed headlong,
> I, misshapen.[12]

And we know his harsh warning:

> How many things craftsmen have made, things without number, employing their manifold skills and ingenuity on apparel, footwear, pottery and artifacts of every conceivable kind, on pictures too, and various images; and how far they have in these matters

exceeded what is reasonably necessary or useful, or serves some pious purpose![13]

This is not a condemnation of art as this saint even tells us to praise God because, despite everything, these images of artistic beauty also come forth from the beauty that is above all. But it certainly is an admonition not to make of them "an opportunity" for the flesh (see Galatians 5:13).

The contemplation of Christ, especially in his Transfiguration, is the most effective antidote to the seduction of beauty. If we are before him often and for long periods, our lips will spontaneously exclaim the words of the psalm, "You are the most handsome of men!" (Psalm 45:2). Fyodor Dostoevsky had tried to represent the ideal of a purely good and positive beauty in his main character in The Idiot, without completely succeeding. Responding to someone who pointed this out, he says, almost as though excusing himself, "There's only one positively beautiful person in the world—Christ, so that the appearance of this measurelessly, infinitely beautiful person is in fact of course an infinite miracle."[14]

When we feel ourselves wounded by images of "carnal" beauty, we should do what the Israelites did in the desert. As soon as they were bitten by poisonous snakes, if they ran to look at the bronze serpent lifted up by Moses, they were healed. Without spending time trying to understand the why and the how in our day (which only gives time for the poison to spread), let us run to the cross or to an icon of the Transfiguration, if we know of one, and gaze upon it. The icon of Christ, and even more so the sacramental Host that contains him, exercises its sanctifying power even through simple sight, if it is accompanied by faith.

Let the healing come to us in precisely the same way the wound came to us, that is, through our eyes! Contemplation has therapeutic power and heals: It is a power for which we have a great need today, since images and entertainment have become the primary vehicle for the world's ideology. The issue is not to avoid looking at anything but to choose what it is we look at. He who created the eye to see also created the eyelid to cover it.

"LET US MAKE THREE DWELLINGS"

Let us turn for a moment to Peter's statement. His suggestion of making three tents has often been interpreted, from Origen on, as a new attempt by the apostle to deflect Jesus from the path toward his Passion, almost as a replica of his earlier "God forbid it, Lord!" (Matthew 16:22).

Saint Augustine gave a different explanation, a perhaps more plausible one. In his view Peter tasted the joy of contemplation and did not wish to return to the distractions and confusion that awaited him below. (In his famous painting *The Transfiguration*, Raphael expressed this contrast, grouping the figures on two levels: on the upper level, at the top of Tabor, Jesus with Moses and Elijah and the three apostles enveloped in light and at peace; on the lower level, at the foot of the mount, a noisy crowd milling around a possessed person.)

Augustine saw in Peter the attitude, not to say temptation, that a bishop who meditates on this Gospel episode can experience. On this point, Augustine's words are particularly timely and relevant:

> He [Peter] was finding the crowds a dreadful bore, he had discovered the solitude of the mountain where he could have Christ to

himself as the bread of the spirit. Why go down there to toil and trouble, while he was experiencing there for God such sacred affection, and hence such virtuous dispositions?[15]

Augustine expresses something here that emerges many times in his writings as a secret lament about his life as a bishop: not to have time for himself to pursue contemplation and study, to be at the beck and call of others night and day, subjected to all kinds of requests that were often anything but spiritual.

What Augustine says here to Peter is what he said to himself and says to every bishop in the same situation:

Come down, Peter: You were eager to go on resting on the mountain; come down, *preach the word, press on in season, out of season, censure, exhort, rebuke in all long-suffering and teaching* (2 Tm 4:2). Toil away, sweat it out, suffer some tortures…. We heard the praises of charity, you see, when the apostle was being read: *It does not seek its own advantage* (1 Cor 13:5)…. He was keeping that [happiness] for you, Peter, after death. But now he says to you, "Go down to labor on earth, to serve on earth, to be despised, crucified on earth."[16]

Contemplation is a good thing, and insofar as it depends on us it is to be preferred to action. However, more important than either is charity. For the sake of charity some may be called to forego activity and others to forego contemplation. It is not exactly a question of foregoing contemplation but of pursuing it under another form. If in fact we cannot or should not be *active in contemplation* (activity, especially of the mind, thwarts true contemplation!), we can and must instead be *contemplatives in action*.

If it is not possible to always remain on Tabor, it is, however, possible to keep Tabor close by. According to her confessor, Saint Catherine of Siena, compelled to be in the world, "made a secret place in her heart by the inspiration of the Holy Spirit from which she would never leave."[17] And when her confessor had to undertake a journey or was burdened by preoccupations, Catherine admonished him with holy freedom, "Make yourself a cell in your own mind from which you can never come out."[18]

If it is possible to carry a cell along with us, it is possible to carry along a mountain. We need to make use of these means with great simplicity and realism. The fact that, according to the Gospel, the kingdom of God is "within us" makes this a reality and not a mental fiction. Right in the middle of our activity, even in a conversation or in a meeting, it is possible, as Saint John of the Cross said at the beginning, to go forth "without being observed" and to climb our interior Tabor. We do not need to withdraw for a long time. One moment suffices, one glance, one thought, to establish beneficial contact with the invisible. Then we can return to listening or to working, better disposed than before, like someone who has adjusted the rudder and then calmly returns to rowing.

"From the Cloud Came a Voice"
According to Heinz Schürmann,

> Immediately God does, in his own way, what Peter wanted to do on a human level: the cloud, a sign of the presence of God and of his glory, "envelops" them. He does not merely gather them under his "shadow" but envelops and protects them in such a way that they can "enter" into it.[19]

This divine tent makes the three tents suggested by Peter useless.

It is true that a cloud is usually associated with the glory of God and is a visible sign of it, but in the New Testament the cloud begins to be associated with the Holy Spirit (see Luke 1:35) and will subsequently be interpreted continuously that way by the Fathers who later comment on the Transfiguration.[20] The cloud in the Transfiguration, then, becomes what the dove is at baptism: the visible sign of the presence of the Holy Spirit. Besides, how could the Spirit be absent in a theophany that is so clearly Trinitarian? He is the space in which the Transfiguration occurs. The very light that radiates from Christ is none other than the Holy Spirit, who was dwelling in his flesh. It was through the operation of the Holy Spirit that the dead body of Christ was reanimated and restored to life in the Resurrection (see Romans 1:4), and he is the same power that shines through Jesus' mortal body on Tabor.

For those of us who approach the Transfiguration for the sake of contemplation, this is an important point. It is not possible to contemplate Jesus except "in the Holy Spirit." In contemplation we become transformed in Christ: "this comes from the Lord, the Spirit," Paul told us (2 Corinthians 3:18). Our confidence rests precisely in this: "We have received...the Spirit that is from God, so that we may understand the gifts bestowed on us by God" (1 Corinthians 2:12)—primarily Jesus, who is the first of all his gifts.

It is the Spirit who reveals an understanding of Christ, his sentiments, his preferences, to the simple. Let us never begin to pray or to contemplate without first invoking the presence of the Spirit: "Come, Creator Spirit. Create in me true prayer, contemplation 'in spirit and in truth.'"

We are approaching the climax of the scene. As in all theophanies, the visible sign—the cloud—is joined by an audible sign, a voice. At Pentecost the visible sign is the tongues of fire, and the audible sign is the sound of the rushing wind. But in this case there is more. The Holy Spirit is present through the visible sign of the cloud, and in the audible sign of the voice, the Father is present and proclaims, "This is my Son, my Chosen; listen to him!" (Luke 9:35).

There were three people in front of the apostles, but the Father does not say, "These are my sons; listen to them!" Instead, he uses the singular: "Listen to him!" Moses and Elijah, the chief spiritual representatives of the Old Testament, are understood now for who they are: In relation to the one who is the Son, they are simple servants in the household of God (see Hebrews 3:2–4).

Traditional iconography has presented this state of affairs in a superb way. The way the icon of the Transfiguration helped me the most spiritually—once I began to appreciate it—is precisely in its depiction of the attitude of Moses and Elijah, arched like bows toward Jesus at the center, displaying an attitude of respectful humility, submission and adoration. Seeing them spontaneously generates in us a desire to imitate them, to be in the presence of Christ the way they are, in completely amazed, grateful, free and joyful submission—just like Mary in some depictions of the Nativity, kneeling before the Son, full of wonder and adoration, just as any creature should do in the presence of the Creator, the servant before his Lord.

"LISTEN TO HIM!"

We know now that when Peter spoke of making three tents he did so "not knowing what he said" (Luke 9:33). To make one tent each for Jesus, Moses and Elijah is to put them all on the same level and to fail to understand the infinite distance that exists between them. The Fathers commented that this also implicitly divides up Scripture, as though Moses and Elijah had spoken in their own names; instead it is the one Word of God speaking through them as well: "The prophets speak, the law speaks, *but this one you must hear*, he being the voice of the law and the tongue of the prophets. He was to be heard in them."[21]

Here the revelation about the person of Jesus as well as the revelation about his place in salvation history reaches its conclusion. On Sinai God had revealed his will for human beings by the giving of the *Torah*: "When God finished speaking with Moses on Mount Sinai, he gave him the two tablets of the covenant, tablets of stone, written with the finger of God" (Exodus 31:18). Later Moses says, "Hear, O Israel, the statutes and ordinances that I am addressing to you today; you shall learn them and observe them diligently" (Deuteronomy 5:1). On Tabor God says, "This is my Son; listen to him!" (Luke 9:35). Christ has taken the place of the Law. It is he, in all that he says and does, who is the definitive and complete expression of the Father's will. He is the future prophet whom Moses had commanded the people to heed (see Deuteronomy 18:15). In the Transfiguration Jesus is far more than the new Moses; he is also the new law. He is not just the new mediator of revelation but also the new and complete self-revelation of God to human beings.

"Listen to him!" How this command of the Father still resonates today! There are two ways we can disobey this command: We can stop short of coming to Christ, or we can go beyond Christ. The danger for us Christians today is obviously the second. However, I am not thinking right now of the danger of syncretism or of philosophies that claim to go "beyond" Christ, in the sense that they hold their system of doctrine—and not the Christian revelation—as the supreme manifestation of the Spirit. I am thinking instead of what Saint John of the Cross said about those for whom the word of Christ is not enough and who always seek new messages and private revelations. To them God could reply,

> Since that day when I descended upon Him with My Spirit on Mount Tabor, saying…. "This is my beloved Son in Whom I am well pleased; hear ye him,"…I have entrusted [all teaching] to him. Hear him; for I have no more faith to reveal, neither have I any more things to declare.[22]

God has now become, in a certain sense, "mute." If we are eager for new revelations and ready to embrace everything that is disseminated through them, we offend him and behave as if he had not told us already through Christ everything that was necessary. As if we did not have enough to do with putting into practice what we already know!

We are living in a time overflowing with heavenly messages of all kinds, which seem to become shriller and more insistent as we enter the new millennium. People no longer wait for the Church's judgment but go ahead and judge for themselves. There are pious people who consider themselves second-class or excluded if they are not in the circle of certain "visionaries." Catholic piety risks becoming disordered again, even after biblical and liturgical movements and the Second Vatican Council in particular tirelessly tried to bring things back to the essentials: the Word of God, the sacraments, the Holy Spirit, charitable works and a sober and healthy devotion to Our Lady.

Bishops and priests can do a lot about this. These messengers with private revelations or apocalyptic prophets know that they need approval from the hierarchy in order to gain a following in Catholic circles. They seek approval and, unfortunately, they sometimes get it. If they do not find it, they invent it for themselves, bragging about oral or written approval and encouragement that they interpret to their own benefit. We cannot always prevent fraud and deceit, but we can warn people in a clearer way than we do now, discouraging them from following after "every wind of doctrine" (Ephesians 4:14).

What motivates many people to accept certain miraculous signs and messages as legitimate is a fear that if they do not, it might look as if they lack faith, or they might be offending God or Our Lady. An ancient desert Father suggests a way to reassure these kinds of people. Imagine, he says, the master of a household who returns home at night after a long absence. He knocks but the servant makes him wait and then refuses to open the door because he is not sure that it is the master outside. Will that master be angry the next morning about the servant's attitude, or will he instead be pleased, seeing how much the servant feared endangering his goods? In the same way God will be pleased when we do not easily believe visions and revelations for fear of welcoming his enemy rather than him.[23]

When authentic mystics and saints received an extraordinary grace or revelation, they needed to be hard-pressed to manifest it. On the other hand, false mystics do not even finish receiving what they believe is a divine message or an extraordinary grace before they are already out the door, restless for the whole world to know.

THEY SAW ONLY JESUS

"When they looked around, they saw no one…but only Jesus" (Mark 9:8). Moses and Elijah have disappeared; the cloud is gone, the voice is silent, and the bright light is gone. Everything has returned to normal. Jesus has also returned to his usual daily appearance. But the very emphasis that all three Synoptic writers give to this final comment (see Matthew 17:18; Mark 9:8; Luke 9:36) conceals a profound significance. It means that this is the Jesus we need to hear, the Jesus of the Gospels, not just the Jesus of exalted moments. The presence of Jesus and his words is enough for the Church. Even the Old Testament from now on will be read above all for one reason: because it speaks of him and he speaks in it. "Moses, the law, and Elijah, the prophet, became one only with the gospel of Jesus; and not, as they were formerly three, did they so abide, but the three became one."[24]

This means that now "we see only Jesus." "Only Jesus": A whole pattern for life is contained in the phrase that concludes the account of the Transfiguration. In theological terms today it would be called the maximum "Christological concentration." Jesus Christ, as anyone can notice in more and more places, has receded in the imagination and language even of Christians today. It is more fashionable to speak generically of "God." Various factors are pushing things in that direction, some of which are good and necessary but some of which are not: inter-religious dialogue, the affirmation of a cosmopolitan mind-set that tends to relativize the differences between religions, not to mention the intolerance toward any kind of religion—such as that of the gospel—that holds to specific standards and behaviors and obedience to the faith and does not leave everything to individual judgment and preference.

"Only Jesus." Of course this does not mean we can dispense with the Father and Holy Spirit, but Jesus is the unique locus in which the Triune God makes himself completely manifest and efficacious for human beings. It means no one goes to the Father except through him, whether they know it or not.

On a personal level, what a way of living is suggested by this expression! There are so many things we can put alongside of Jesus in our lives: Jesus and money, Jesus and one's career, Jesus and one's freedom, Jesus and the consolations he brings. Making the cry of "Only Jesus!" resonate in our own spirits is like throwing a rock at a tree swarming with birds that are making a great racket. Our thoughts, projects and useless preoccupations fly away like birds, and a wonderful silence and peace settle into our hearts.

It is written that when Moses came down from Mount Sinai, he did not know that his face was shining "because he had been talking with God" (Exodus 34:29). Descending from our Tabor now to return to daily tasks, let us hope that our faces too—without our being aware of it—transmit some of the peace and serenity given to us by what we contemplated on the holy mount.

CHAPTER 3

I WANT TO KNOW CHRIST

On Tabor With Paul

THE CHRIST WHO EMBRACES ALL TIMES AND AGES

Today we will ascend Tabor and pursue our contemplation of the transfigured Christ guided by the apostle Paul. In describing the apostle's depiction of Christ, I am taking a synthetic rather than an analytic approach. In other words, I would like to review quickly three of Paul's most famous and dense Christological texts, in the order in which they were written, to trace the development in Paul of a full and definitive image of Christ. It takes boldness to tackle all three texts in such a restricted space, since each has had whole books written about it, but there are certain aspects of these texts that can be seen only by an overview of the whole, only by synthesis rather than by analysis.

The first of these famous texts is Romans 1:1–4. There Paul says he was set apart for

> the gospel of God, which he *promised* beforehand through his
> prophets in the holy scriptures, the gospel concerning his Son, who

> was *descended* from David according to the flesh and was *declared*
> to be Son of God with power according to the spirit of holiness
> by resurrection from the dead, Jesus Christ our Lord. (emphasis
> added)

It is generally said that this text has a *binary* structure insofar as it presents the life of Christ at two times or in two phases: the earthly Jesus, according to the flesh, and the glorified Jesus, according to the Spirit. However, it is really a *three-part* text that presents a picture of Christ at three different times. The same Christ is contemplated first as "promised," then as "descended" (or born) and finally as "exalted" ("declared to be the Son of God with power").

To go right to the heart of the matter, what does this text say about Jesus? It says that Jesus Christ is present throughout the whole history of salvation, that he occupies all of it and not just a part: first in the Old Testament as *promised*, then in the fullness of time as *having come* and finally in the time of the Church age as *believed in*. Everything belongs to him. In the words that accompany the lighting of the paschal candle, "all time... and all the ages"[1] are all truly his.

To regard the Old Testament as a time also belonging to Christ is the common assumption of all the authors of the New Testament. The one who spoke through the prophets was "the Spirit of Christ" (1 Peter 1:11). Abraham saw Jesus' day (see John 8:56), and Moses contemplated his glory (see Exodus 33:18–23). Jesus himself said the Scriptures "testify on my behalf" (John 5:39).

The "promise of the gospel" is already, in a certain sense, the gospel, even if it is still shrouded in "shadows and images." The Law, the Fathers used to say, was "pregnant with Christ." For that reason we cannot lay aside the Old Testament, even after the gospel has come. That would be like wanting to eliminate the nine months spent inside the womb from a person's life. It is true that those months are not used to calculate a person's age (which is only calculated from birth), but who would dare say that they do not belong to or are not important for a person's life?

This is the justification for a typological reading of the Old Testament, initiated by Christ himself, followed by the apostles and subsequently always preached by the Church. To say that the Old Testament is a "type" and "figure" does not downgrade it or empty it of meaning but instead promotes it. This does not take away from its historical reality and substance, as one might fear, because preserving the historicity and full reality of the facts of the Old Testament adds a prophetic value to them. What an ancient axiom said of the Word that was incarnated can also be said of the Old Testament: "In becoming what he was not, he did not cease to be what he was."[2] Fire loses nothing of its splendor when it becomes a symbol for the Holy Spirit; instead it acquires a new nobility.

In this light we can understand another important truth: In the eyes of a Christian the Jews are not entirely deprived of Jesus Christ because they possess the Scriptures that contain him. The Christ "promised beforehand...in the holy Scriptures" is the one who objectively unites us with the Jewish people. He is the silent but strongest bond of all. Jesus walks with them as he walked with the two disciples of Emmaus before they recognized him. He is the cornerstone that unites the two sides of the building, the two testaments.

The faith of the Fathers was, in this sense, much bolder than ours. Irenaeus, for example, writes, "The Son of God is implanted everywhere throughout his [Moses'] writings.... If anyone, therefore, reads the Scriptures with attention, he will find in them an account of Christ, and a foreshadowing of the new calling."[3]

In Paul's mind Christ has assumed that dimension already! This text from Romans contains everything that was highlighted in books like *Christ and Time* by Oscar Cullman.[4] Christ does not occupy only a segment of history and of time—even if he is "the central point of time"—he occupies all of it. He is the backbone of history; without him time would be "spineless." He redeems the past from emptiness and the future from unreality. The past, as time, no longer exists, but Christ, who fills the past, still remains; the future is not yet, but Christ, who will fill the future, exists already.

"THOUGH HE WAS IN THE FORM OF GOD"

Let us see what is added to this picture of Christ—already presented in such vast dimensions—by the second great Christological text from Paul, which is in the Letter to the Philippians:

> Let the same mind be in you that was in Christ Jesus,
>> who, though he was in the form of God,
>>> did not regard equality with God
>>> as something to be exploited,
>> but emptied himself,
>>> taking the form of a slave,
>>> being born in human likeness.
>> And being found in human form,
>>> he humbled himself
>>> and became obedient to the point of death—
> even death on a cross.

Therefore God also highly exalted him
and gave him the name
that is above every name,
so that at the name of Jesus
every knee should bend,
in heaven and on earth and under the earth,
and every tongue should confess
that Jesus Christ is Lord,
to the glory of God the Father. (Philippians 2:5–11)

This text, written after the preceding one, shows us how Christ "is growing" in Paul's understanding and how his faith is becoming deeper and more fervent as time goes on. In this text, Christ is no longer confined to history as though enclosed by it but transcends it. He comes from outside of time and he goes beyond time. The earlier frameworks—the Old Testament, the time of Jesus, the time of the Church—are no longer present. Instead the framework here is "a divine world and a human world," "eternity and time," seen concretely as stages of existence and not abstractly as metaphysical categories.

Paul highlights all this through the mention of the three "forms" in which Christ was clothed: the form of God, the form of a servant and the form of the Lord. Jesus Christ unites within himself not only the three *ages* of history but even eternity and time. With his *kenosis* (self-emptying) in the Incarnation, eternity entered time, and with his glorification in the Resurrection, time entered eternity. This is precisely what has been defined as the "paradox" of Christ.[5]

What lies beneath the text from Romans is a *diachronic* vision, that is, a vision that moves from one time to another; it unfolds in time. (In music a diachronic scale sounds the notes separately one after another.) The underlying vision in this text from Philippians is a *metachronic* vision: It goes beyond time.

But apart from these descriptive attempts, what does this second text offer that is new theologically? A decisive point: It says that our salvation comes from God and rests in God, that it is secure. This resolves the question of whether Christian salvation is a gift or an achievement, whether people save themselves or are saved by God. If the Savior were to come from Earth, there is no way to avoid saying that salvation comes just from Earth, for "the one who is of the earth belongs to the earth" (John 3:31). This goes back to the great Gnostic myth of the "redeemed redeemer," of the savior who first needs to be saved before he can save others.

We need to be very clear on this point: The Jubilee of 2000 did not commemorate the absolute beginning of the history of Jesus Christ. His birth in the world is not like other births; it is the beginning of his manifestation in the flesh but not of his being.

THE COSMIC CHRIST

The third great Christological "hymn" is from Colossians 1:15–20. The layout below helps to highlight Paul's three-part presentation.

1. He is the image of the invisible God, the firstborn of all creation.

2. For in him all things in heaven and on earth were created, things visible and invisible, whether thrones or dominions or rulers or powers—all things have been created through him and for him. He himself is before all things, and in him all things hold together.

3. He is the head of the body, the Church; he is the beginning, the firstborn from the dead, so that he might come to have first place in everything. For in him all the fullness of God was pleased to dwell, and through him God was pleased to reconcile to himself all things, whether on earth or in heaven, by making peace through the blood of his cross.

This passage reflects the "understanding of the mystery of Christ" (Ephesians 3:4) that Paul attained toward the end of his life.

Before developing some reflections on it, I would like to offer an observation. All three "hymns" I am discussing here are considered "pre-Pauline" by many scholars, that is, preexisting texts that the apostle would have found, perhaps in the Church's liturgy, and inserted into his epistles.

On the premise that the inspired authority of these texts is not in question in any way, I need to express a growing doubt I have. There are dozens of texts in the Pauline *corpus* that have now been declared, by one exegete or another, as liturgical, baptismal or Gnostic, that is, pre-Pauline. There is not one section that differs a bit from the rest and has some kind of metrical progression—real or imagined—that has not been removed from Paul's authorship. This hypothesis, after being applied to one initial case (in Philippians), has been extended to other texts. One now has the impression that everyone who uses this hypothesis regards it as evidence already demonstrated by some previous author. Meanwhile, no one explains the arguments on which this hypothesis is based, and when they are set forth they seem extremely flimsy.

I would like to briefly mention certain facts that should lead to more caution in this regard. The hymnlike characteristic of these passages is exaggerated and in some cases depends merely on a current practice of formatting them to look like poetry. The majority of them can be very easily read as normal prose passages from a Jewish writer who has the slightest familiarity with the technique of parallelism. But even if they were authentic hymns, who says that everybody at that time knew how to write hymns except Paul and John? Furthermore, since they deal with powerful syntheses and with texts that are among the most profound and brilliant of the New Testament, we have to ask ourselves, "Who are these geniuses who sprang up at the heart of the community in less than twenty years? What happened to them? Can it be possible that they left no other traces of themselves?" We are familiar with some passages in liturgical texts from the *Didache* and other writings from the earliest times, but there is no trace of these Christological texts that were supposedly used by the early Church. Not only that, but what we do find in those other passages, such as "the holy vine of David," is of very mediocre quality in comparison to the Christological hymns, which reflect a more advanced stage of faith.[6]

To claim that the Christological hymns in the New Testament texts are preexisting has become, I believe, a fashionable trend that is still being propagated uncritically, and it is based on questionable internal criteria. Suffice it to say there is not one author who concurs with another in determining which elements of a text have been changed and which have been added by Paul. It is not easy to imagine a man like Paul inserting whole passages known to his readers into his writings without minimally acknowledging it or justifying such insertions. In Ephesians 5:14, where he does quote from a preexisting hymn, he introduces it with the formula "it says." I believe one encounters only very minor difficulties in accepting the above texts as genuinely Pauline.

With this premise, we come to our last text. What does the hymn in Colossians add to what Saint Paul has already told us about Christ? The perspective here is not so much historical as ontological and cosmic. Christ is not seen against the background of salvation history, according to a "time-eternity" pattern, but against the background of all of reality and the cosmos. If in the text from Romans the perspective is *diachronic,* and in Philippians it is *metachronic,* here it is *synchronic.* (In music a synchronic scale is one in which all the basic notes are heard together in harmony.) Christ is considered simultaneously here in his threefold "relationship": with God, with the cosmos and with humanity.

With respect to God, Christ is his "image" and his "firstborn." With respect to the cosmos, "all things have been created through him and for him" (Colossians 1:16). With respect to humanity and the Church, he is the "head," the one who has reconciled all things to God. In other words, not only all of *history* but also all of *reality* belongs to Christ and is submitted to him.

Some Christological passages from the Letter to the Ephesians complete this vision, saying that within humanity and within the Church both Jews and gentiles belong to Christ because he made one people out of the two groups, namely, the Church (see Ephesians 2:14–18). Paul considers this last point as the special message entrusted to him, the "hidden mystery" that has now been made manifest: "The Gentiles have become fellow heirs, members of the same body" (see Ephesians 3:5–6).

Thus the maximal extension of Jesus' sphere of authority has been achieved. Truly God has placed "everything" under his feet.

Nothing and no one, much less the gentiles, can be lawfully removed from his lordship without thereby excluding them from salvation as well.

Sometimes the question arises as to what we should think about the theory that is becoming more prevalent in scientific circles about the existence of intelligent beings in other parts of the universe. If that turned out to be true, wouldn't that force us to correct a cosmic vision of Christ like Paul's? I am personally convinced that this would absolutely not be the case. The existence of extraterrestrial beings in fact would not change the substance of things. It would merely be a question of drawing out the ultimate implications from our faith in Christ and from history.

Were the inhabitants of America, before the news of Christ arrived, in an essentially different position than that of the hypothetical inhabitants of other planets? If there are other intelligent human beings in the universe, either they already know the Savior—even if under another name—or they are waiting to know him, and we need to make him known. *Ite in mundum universum:* "Go into all the world" (Mark 16:15), including that one too.

I cannot reflect on Paul's faith without feeling moved with admiration and emotion. I was in Athens one day for a preaching engagement. It was the first time I had set foot in Greece. The first thing I wanted to do was to go to the Areopagus. There I reread the account from Acts of the Apostles that was written on a bronze plaque affixed to a rock.

One thing in particular struck me. Shortly after the pagan scholars of Athens refused the gospel, Paul wrote the Letter to the Romans, in Corinth. In the introduction he calmly asserted that he had received the grace of apostleship "to bring about the obedience of faith among all Gentiles" (Romans 1:5). *Obedience* and, furthermore, of *all* gentiles! His failure in Athens did not in the least affect the certitude that he had derived from knowing "who" Jesus is. It is precisely the understanding that he now had of Christ—or better, that had been revealed to him by the Father—that gave him this unshakable certainty.

I said to myself, "If only we had a small seed of Paul's faith today! We would not let ourselves be intimidated by the fact that much of the world still needs to be evangelized and still refuses, sometimes disdainfully like the Areopagites, to let itself be evangelized. We would truly have what we need to undertake a new evangelization." But that can only happen if a Jesus Christ of cosmic dimensions, like the one who lived in Paul, lives in us through faith.

After Athens, I visited Corinth. And there in the place where the Jews brought Paul to Gallio (see Acts 18:12–17), I had the same feeling. In that *agora* ("marketplace") in Corinth the apostle reached out to the people and made the first disciples. At that moment the immense burden of carrying the gospel to all peoples still lay ahead. Wouldn't it have seemed an impossible goal? But Paul said, "I know the one in whom I have put my trust" (2 Timothy 1:12), and two thousand years have vindicated the boldness of his faith. This is a strong incentive for us to stake everything, absolutely everything, on Jesus, whether on a spiritual or an intellectual level, convinced that there exists nothing and no one in the universe that is "above" Christ.

THE PATH OF FAITH

I said that Paul sets forth one of the two fundamental ways of approaching the mystery of Christ. Let us summarize the particular characteristics of this path that will cause it to become a

Christological example and archetype in the development of Christian thought.

This path

- goes from Christ's *humanity* to his *divinity*, from his history to his preexistence. It is, therefore, an ascending path. It follows the sequence of Christ's *manifestation*, the sequence in which men have known him, not the sequence of his *being*. (Even in the text from Colossians, the one who is described as "the image of the invisible God" is the historical Christ, the Redeemer!).

- goes from Christ's *duality* (flesh and Spirit) to the *unity* of his person as "Jesus Christ our Lord."

- has the *paschal mystery* at its center, that is, Christ's *action* rather than his *person*. The great turning point between the two phases of the existence of Christ is his *resurrection* from the dead.

To make sure this is not simply our modern reconstruction, we can glance ahead quickly to see how these characteristics will be received and developed in the sub-apostolic generation, the generation of disciples that followed the apostles. As early as with Saint Ignatius of Antioch, flesh and Spirit—the two *phases* of the life of Christ (before and after the Resurrection)—will point to the two *births* of Jesus, from Mary and from God. They will ultimately point to the two *natures* of Christ: "The apostle, too, teaches in this way about the duality of substance. He writes, 'who came to be the seed of David' (this will mean the human being and the Son of man), and then 'who was shown to be the Son of God according to the Spirit'...(this will mean God and the Word of God, his Son)."[7]

Paul inaugurated a path that was destined to develop a determinative role in deepening our understanding of the mystery of Christ. But this path is to be lived rather than studied, and that is what we would like to do now, or at least try to do. What is the most important response that a person can have—the decision that he or she should make—to Christ as the apostle has "publicly exhibited" (Galatians 3:1) him to us? The appropriate response is "to believe"! We can call Paul's path "the path of faith."

One needs to believe above all in the *action* of Christ, in the salvific event of his death and resurrection. The paschal mystery is at the heart of everything. In the Pauline vision we achieve salvation by proclaiming that Jesus is Lord and believing that God raised him from the dead (see Romans 10:9), that is, by accepting the paschal mystery. At one point, the apostle exclaims, "I want to know Christ." What does he want to know about him? "The power of his resurrection," he answers, "and the sharing of his sufferings" (Philippians 3:10). Invariably, everything brings us back to the paschal mystery.

With this kind of faith one enters into the sphere of Christ's action not only intellectually but also mystically, so that one becomes a "new creature" and begins to live "in Christ Jesus" (1 Corinthians 1:30). All of this transpires "in the Holy Spirit." It is thanks to the Holy Spirit that one has faith and thanks to faith that one has the Holy Spirit (see Galatians 3:2; 5:5).

"FORGETTING WHAT LIES BEHIND"

When the most creative era of theology, the age of the Fathers, ended, the Christological models tended to become detached from reality and to be handled like technical formulas, often polemically against other formulas, without any serious personal involvement. That is the danger of formalism. That is certainly not the way it is with Saint Paul. He is giving expression to a lived experience. His Christological "model" has a soul. It is enough to reread the most autobiographical passage in all of his writings, Philippians 3:5–14, to be convinced about that.

This passage must be considered, for all practical purposes, a "Christological" text. It completes the picture delineated by the three preceding hymns, no longer highlighting who Christ is "in himself" in relation to God, to time, to the world and to humanity in general, but who he is "for me," for every individual believer. This is the soul of the Pauline path: the point at which the mystical encounter between Christ and the believer occurs. Paul's path is not merely an objective path, but also a subjective one—not merely theological but existential.

The encounter with Christ divided Paul's life in two; it changed the meaning and value of everything for him. His earlier reasons for confidence and pride—he belonged to the elect people and, furthermore, to its most zealous sect, the Pharisees; he was observant of the Law and irreproachable—were suddenly lost, became rubbish, "because of...Christ Jesus my Lord" (Philippians 3:8). He does not say "our Lord" but "my" Lord. A personal relationship has been established between himself and Jesus. For Paul the "surpassing value of knowing" Jesus is the highest, most necessary and most beatifying kind of knowing possible. "Christ Jesus has made me his own [taken hold of me]" (Philippians 3:12): Paul explains everything by these words.

From this passage it is also clear that the relationship with Christ is not something static, settled once and for all at the beginning, at conversion. It is a relationship that must always be renewed and that, in turn, renews and rejuvenates everything else. "Forgetting what lies behind…, I press on towards the goal" (Philippians 3:13–14). What "lies behind" for him? The past that he spoke about earlier of being a Pharisee? No, the past of being an apostle in the Church! Now the "gain" to be considered as "loss" is something else: It is precisely having already once considered everything to be a loss because of Christ. It would be natural to think, "What courage Paul has! He abandoned a rabbinic career that was thriving for an obscure group of Galileans! And what letters he wrote! How many journeys he took and how many churches he founded!"

The apostle indirectly warned against the mortal danger of placing "his own justification" based on works (this time works done for Christ) between Christ and himself and reacted vigorously: "I have [not] already obtained" perfection, he says, or "already reached the goal" (Philippians 3:12). Saint Francis of Assisi, in a similar situation, cut off every temptation to self-complacency in saying, "Let us begin, brothers, to serve the Lord God, for up till now we have made little or no progress."[8]

This echoes an evangelical teaching. The apostles had left all for Christ, but each one had received a small patrimony, this time based on merit. One could claim that he followed Jesus first; another, that he had been entrusted with the common purse; still another, that he had been promised the primacy. One day as they discussed among themselves who was the greatest in the kingdom of the heaven, Jesus said to them, "Truly I tell you, unless you change and become like little children, you will never enter the kingdom of heaven" (Matthew 18:3). In addition to not being the greatest, there is the danger of not entering the kingdom of heaven at all!

This is the "second conversion," the one for those who have already followed Christ and have served him in the Church. It is a very particular kind of conversion because it does not consist in leaving behind evil but, in a certain sense, in leaving behind the good! It consists in detaching oneself from everything one has done, repeating to oneself, according to Christ's suggestion, "We are worthless slaves; we have done only what we ought to have done" (Luke 17:10).

Right to the end of Paul's life, therefore, Christ is for him the spiritual mainspring, the one who keeps his spirit young and fresh and makes him capable of new endeavors and new initiatives, "forgetting what lies behind and straining forward to what lies ahead" (Philippians 3:13). In his old age, after so many experiences, tireless efforts and conflicts, Paul is still enthusiastic about Christ. We should say to him, "Thank you, brother Paul! Your example makes us want to choose Jesus again as Lord of our lives, to let go again of everything that tries to cling to us and ensnare us, for the sake of a new adventure with Christ. You make us want to cry out with you, 'For to me, living is Christ' (Philippians 1:21)."

CHAPTER 4

IN THE BEGINNING WAS THE WORD

On Tabor With John

Mountain paths that lead to certain peaks like the Matterhorn or Everest are named after the first mountain climber who marked them. The same is true for the paths that take us to spiritual Tabor, the summit where Christ is contemplated. These paths also have names and, having spoken about "Paul's path," I would like to describe "John's path." To follow these two paths sequentially shows us how we can still reach Christ today coming from different vantage points, with different diction and from diverse cultural backgrounds, as long as that occurs, of course, within the great riverbed of Scripture and Tradition. The ancients said of God, "Not by one avenue only can we arrive at so tremendous a secret."[1] And that saying applies to Christ as well.

THE PROLOGUE

John also summarized his whole vision of the mystery of Christ in a "hymn," the prologue to his Gospel. The prologue is like the prelude in an opera that introduces the "themes," the "motifs" and the "arias" that will be developed during the course of that piece. John's is not only a *prologue* but also an *epilogue:* It can be read either at the beginning or at the conclusion of his Gospel.

This hymn is also said to have preexisted the author of the fourth Gospel, who is said to have adapted it. That changes nothing for our purposes. According to C.H. Dodd, "When the Fourth Gospel was published and received by the Church, the prologue stood as an integral part of it. It is for us to interpret it as such."[2]

However, I believe the same premise I observed about Paul needs to be repeated here. Where is this genius who would have composed a hymn like this? Is it possible that there is also no trace of him in literature or history? And is it conceivable that this Gospel writer, who is certainly not merely an imitator of others, would place a very long passage at the beginning of his Gospel that his readers—or at least the majority of them—would recognize without giving any indication of that? Since, as I said, the prologue seems to be a summary of and a prelude to the whole Gospel, we would need either to conclude that this Gospel writer conceived of his work as a development of and commentary on an existing hymn that was unrelated to the Christian faith (an exceedingly unlikely theory) or to conclude that the person who composed the hymn was someone who was familiar with and wanted to summarize John's Gospel.

The fact that the word *logos* appears only in the prologue does not pose a real problem either, or if it does, it does so whether John composed it or not. Throughout this Gospel the evangelist often reuses the terms *life* and *light*, which are part of the supposedly preexisting hymn as well. What, therefore, would prevent him, if he had wanted to, from also using the term *logos* again? The fact that *logos* is found only in the prologue does not mean that John did not write it; otherwise, we would have to say that chapters fourteen though sixteen in that Gospel are not from John because the title *Paraclete* appears only in those chapters.

This kind of approach opens the door to an unverifiable and arbitrary manipulation of texts. This is demonstrated by the fact that no author agrees with another in determining which elements of the hymn are preexisting and which have been added by the Gospel writer. The prologue ends up being a section with "inserts," in which all the scattered mentions of John the Baptist would be wedged in by the Gospel writer. When one ventures down this road in handling ancient texts, experience has shown that one ends up getting carried away and lost in a tangle of hypotheses.

But apart from these philological issues, to whom can we attribute a text like this that reverberates from one end to the other with a lived experience and an enthusiasm that only an encounter with a real person can cause? "We have seen his glory!" (John 1:14). This is the same experience reported at the beginning of the First Letter of John: "What we have heard, what we have seen with our eyes, what we have looked at and touched with our hands, concerning the word of life…we declare to you" (1 John 1:1, 3).

No one denies that terms and themes that were widespread in various religious circles of the Jewish and Hellenic worlds are conflated in the prologue. But I believe that was done after due consideration and with a very clear goal in mind. The Gospel writer has embraced themes, symbols and expectations—all that was most religiously relevant in his environment—to demonstrate their fulfillment in Christ. He learned the "lingo" of the people in his time to proclaim, with all his might, the one and only truth that saves, the Word par excellence.

Since antiquity the Church has grasped the extraordinary importance of this text and has had a special veneration for it, treating it almost like a relic. Saint Augustine refers favorably to the thinking of a philosopher in his day, Simplicianus, according to whom John's prologue "was fit to be written in letters of gold, and set up to be read in the highest places of all churches."[3] Up until a few years ago, the prologue was written on a special placard on the altar and was read at the end of each Mass. Now it is kept only for Christmas. Proclaimed during the third Mass of Christmas, called "Mass During the Day," it constitutes the end of Advent and is a beacon that illuminates the whole Christmas season. It also announces the paschal mystery: "He came to what was his own, and his own people did not accept him" (John 1:11).

THE WORD, GOD, COSMOS AND HUMANITY

In the prologue, especially at the beginning, we can find a few elements that outline John's "path":

1.   In the beginning was the Word,
2.   and the Word was with God,
3.   and the Word was God. (John 1:1)

The subject John begins with here is the Word-God. John has already reached the ultimate conclusion.

In the process of ascending the mountain in search of the "beginning" of the history of Jesus, we find an interesting progression: The most ancient writers start from the *resurrection* of the dead to tell the story of Christ; with Mark, the "beginning" of the Gospel shifts to the *baptism* of Jesus in the Jordan (see Mark 1:1), while in the other two Synoptic Gospel writers, Matthew and Luke, the beginning is moved back to the *earthly birth* of Christ. Lastly, John comes and makes a decisive leap, placing the "beginning" before time, in Christ's *eternal birth* from God.

The prologue considers the *Logos* in relation to God, the cosmos and humanity, in that order. With respect to God, he is his Word, equal to him ("God") yet distinct from him ("with God"). With respect to the cosmos, he is the means by which all things have been created (see John 1:3). With respect to humanity, he is the "light" and "life" (John 1:4) and, at the same time, a human being in the flesh as we are: "And the Word became flesh and lived among us" (John 1:14).

At this point, there is the impression of something coming down, of falling down to Earth. In the Old Testament, there is mention of a word of God that "falls" (see Isaiah 9:8) or "rests" on Israel (see Zechariah 9:1) as if referring to something material that has weight and substance. In this case, it is not a word, but "the Word" that has fallen and rests not only on Israel but on the whole world.

Let us proceed to the "finale" of the prologue: "The law indeed was given through Moses; grace and truth came through Jesus Christ" (John 1:17).

Only here at the end is the name of Jesus Christ finally pronounced. The name identifies the new subject that from now on will be the focus of all the rest of the Gospel: Becoming flesh, the *Logos* became Jesus Christ.

As we saw in the hymn from Colossians, Paul likewise considered Christ in his tripartite relationship: with God, of whom he is called the "image," with the cosmos and with humanity. What is the difference, then, that allows us to speak of two distinct paths? There is a difference, and it is a big one. Paul starts from the very place where John ends, that is, from Jesus Christ the historical being, through whom we have received redemption and the remission of sins. This leads to another difference: The people spoken of in John's prologue are not yet "the Church," while the people in Paul's text from Colossians are.

Thus we can already indicate, in contrast to Paul's path, the characteristics of this second path of ascent to Christ. This path

- goes from *divinity* to *humanity*. The pattern is inverted here: It is no longer "flesh-Spirit" but "*Logos*-flesh." It is not first the human, the visible, and then the divine, the invisible, but the opposite. John begins from the vantage point of Christ's being—not of Christ's manifestation to us—and from that vantage point it is clear that divinity precedes humanity in Christ.
- goes from *unity* to *duality: Logos* and flesh, divinity and humanity. In language used later on, this path departs from the *person* to arrive at the *natures*.
- focuses on the *Incarnation*, not the *Resurrection* or the paschal mystery, as the great divide—the pivot point around which everything revolves. In addition, the Incarnation is not seen as a *kenosis*, a self-emptying, but, on the contrary as a new phase of the glory of the divine Word: "We have seen his glory" (John 1:14).

The person of Christ is emphasized more than his action, his *being* rather than his *doing*, including the paschal mystery of death and resurrection. This last act essentially functions to reveal who Jesus is: "When you have lifted up the Son of Man, then you will realize that I am he" (John 8:28).

It is also worthwhile here to glance ahead to the sub-apostolic generation, the first successors of the apostles. These two ways of speaking of Christ are clearly delineated by them and help us, at the same time, to try to harmonize them and correlate Paul's pattern of "flesh-Spirit" with John's "*Logos*-flesh." "Christ," says one of those Fathers, "became flesh (even though he was originally spirit)."[4] The order, as we can see, is reversed here. It is not first the flesh, then the Spirit—after the Resurrection—but first the Spirit and then the flesh—after the Incarnation. Paul's point of departure was Christ's humanity, but John's is divinity. The moment of transition from one status to the other, which was the Resurrection for Paul, is the Incarnation for John.

However, despite these differences, there is a profound affinity and reciprocal connection between these paths, so we can proceed in either direction. For both Paul and John, Jesus Christ is true God and true man (flesh) and is one and indivisible. For he is both the *Redeemer* and *revealer* for the whole world, even if Paul emphasizes the redeemer and John emphasizes the revealer. For both, our relation to Christ is mediated and made possible by the Holy Spirit. It is by believing in Christ, they both say, that one receives the Spirit (see Galatians 3:2; John 7:39), and it is by receiving the Spirit that one is able to believe in Christ (see 1 Corinthians 12:3; John 6:63).

The paths of Paul and John have this above all in common: In either path, it is the Holy Spirit who is the "vector," the guide, the one who allows us to walk these paths. Furthermore, this is not just an *idea* they share, but it is an *experience* they both have lived. Speaking of the unique "understanding of the mystery of

Christ" he was granted, Saint Paul says that this mystery "has now been revealed to his holy apostles and prophets by the Spirit" (Ephesians 3:4–5). John, for his part, affirms that it is the Paraclete who testifies to Christ and leads the disciples into all the truth about him (see John 16:13–15).

THIS IS THE WAY, WALK IN IT!

In the prophet Isaiah we read, "Your ears shall hear a word behind you, saying, 'This is the way, walk in it'" (Isaiah 30:21). That same invitation is extended to us today. We have reconstructed the path to Christ outlined by John; all that remains now is for us to walk in it.

What is the step to take, the decision to make, before the Jesus John depicts? Again, to believe! But believe what? Here is the new dimension in John: to believe not so much in what Jesus "has done" for us—his paschal mystery—but in who he "is." To believe "in him," to believe "in his name," that is, in his very person, and thereby to enter into communion with the Father (see 1 John 1:3).

To believe is to "receive" the Word. The drama of the prologue focuses precisely on this "receiving." It is here that the discernment and separation of spirits occur. Humanity is divided into two groups: those who have received and those who have not received the light of the Word: "He came to what was his own, and his own people did not accept him. But to all who received him, who believed in his name, he gave power to become children of God" (John 1:11–12).

It is quite natural for us to group ourselves with those who have received the Word. And thanks be to God, that is true. But the line of demarcation, in this case, is completely unique. It does not merely divide people into two categories—believers and unbelievers—but it also draws a line of demarcation within each individual: between what already belongs to the "new self" in us and lives according to the Spirit, and what still belongs to the "old self" (see Ephesians 4:22–24). Faith and unbelief coexist in every human being.

John's prologue always spurs us to make an examination of conscience: "Have I really received the Word?" If "to receive" simply meant to believe, to adhere mentally, to give assent to faith, I think we could all answer yes. But "to receive" means something more here. The Benedictine monk Célestin Charlier, a passionate spiritual commentator on the prologue, said,

> We know the Word has come among us, but how do we respond to his coming? Do we really pay attention?… Not to make complete and total room for him means to misunderstand him. The coming of the Son of God to human beings is invasive and demands all the attention of our hearts…. It should shape our lives and dictate all our conduct. If this does not happen, we ourselves are those of "his own people" who did not recognize him.[5]

In the World But Not of It

Let us take up another nudge or challenge from reading the prologue. At the center of John's vision of Christ is the Incarnation, as we have seen. It is essential that we really understand the concept of incarnation in John because it has been accepted as a paradigm by the Church every time she speaks of the Christian's duty on earth. *Gaudium et Spes* rightly cites John 1:14, "And the Word was made flesh," when illustrating the relationship between the Church and the world.[6]

One thing strikes us immediately in reading the prologue and then all of the fourth Gospel: John is the one who most emphasizes the Word's *entering* into the world and, at the same time, is the one who insists the most on Christ's *distancing* himself from the world to the point of his disturbing statement, "I do not pray for the world" (see John 17:9). What did he mean by that? That the *Incarnation* is completely other than *becoming worldly*. There is an irreconcilable opposition between the two: One negates the other. It is necessary to go into the world but without becoming worldly.

This is what the Epistle to Diognetus calls "the remarkable and admittedly unusual character" of Christians' lives: They live like everyone else and yet are distinguishable from everyone else.[7] This is merely the continuation of the state of affairs inaugurated by Christ himself. He "came into the world," and "was in the world," but he did not "belong to the world," nor was his kingdom of this world (see John 1:9–10; 17:16; 18:36).

Some people think that since the Council we have found ourselves in an ambiguous situation with regard to this issue because people no longer speak, as they once did, of the *fuga mundi* ("the flight from the world"). In fact, the flight *from* the world seems to have been substituted in some cases by a flight *into* the world. There may be some truth to that, but I believe that the problem is more radical and that the danger of becoming worldly now operates on a deeper level than that. Looking back on the history of the Church, we can discover examples of extreme worldliness in eras during which there was a lot of talk about a "flight from the world"; people wrote treatises by that title, and everyone considered it an undisputable ideal.

Precisely the worst thing would be to condemn the world and then to imitate it secretly, to condemn it verbally but then to imitate it in thought, judgments and actions. This is what laypeople often reprove us clergy for, and they are not always mistaken. Another incongruity would be to expect that the world would listen to us through its powerful information media and agree with us at the very moment we claim the right to denounce its sin. The world approves those who approve it and rejects those who reject it. Otherwise it would mean that it is already converted, that it has believed in Jesus and is, therefore, no longer the "world" in the gospel sense.

T.S. Eliot writes,

In a world of fugitives
The person taking the opposite direction
Will appear to run away.[8]

This is what happens to a Christian in the world. That person is, by definition, someone who is "taking the opposite direction"; a "converted person" is someone who goes against the current. The pagans, Peter writes to the Christians, "are surprised that you no longer join them in the same excesses of dissipation, and so they blaspheme" (1 Peter 4:4).

But earlier still, it is Jesus who says to his disciples,

If the world hates you, be aware that it hated me before it hated you. If you belonged to the world, the world would love you as its own. Because you do not belong to the world, but I have chosen you out of the world—therefore the world hates you. Remember the word that I said to you, "Servants are not greater than their master." (John 15:18–20)

A maxim attributed to Gregory the Great says, *Corruptio optimi pessima*: "The best, when it is corrupted, becomes the worst." Even the principle of the Incarnation, when misunderstood, becomes the worst if it becomes *worldliness*, which is the very negation of that tension between light and darkness, between faith and unbelief, that permeates the prologue and the whole fourth Gospel from beginning to end. Worldliness is the real "hidden evil" in the Church and particularly in religious orders; through it the "salt" loses its savor (see Matthew 5:13; Mark 9:50; Luke 14:34–35).

I was saying, however, that the real problem of worldliness is found at a more widespread and profound level than that of ideologies and theologies. It is situated in the heart of the Christian. It is a danger that is always ready to ensnare us. If we look at past failings, it is only so we can be more attentive today.

Saint John himself lists for us the points for this examination of conscience:

> Do not love the world or the things in the world. The love of the Father is not in those who love the world; for all that is in the world—the desire of the flesh, the desire of the eyes, the pride in riches—comes not from the Father but from the world. (1 John 2:15–16)

Worldliness means to be contented with the desire of the flesh, the desire of the eyes and pride. If there were ever any doubt once as to what the "desire of the eyes" means, I believe there is no longer any doubt about it today. We live in a culture that has made the image its preferred weapon of seduction, its most efficient vehicle for a worldly mentality saturated with sensuality and violence.

A healthy fast from images is indispensable in cultivating the life of the spirit and in avoiding dissipation. The best way to overcome the power of seduction through images is to "look not at what can be seen but at what cannot be seen" (2 Corinthians 4:18). If you look at certain images, they have already won their victory over you. The only thing they want from you is that you look at them.

THE DISCIPLE WHOM JESUS LOVED AND WHO LOVED JESUS

John's contemplation of Christ offers us not only a challenge to make an examination of conscience but also a strong incentive to rediscover the person of Jesus and to renew our living relationship with him. John himself demonstrates in an extraordinary way the power that Jesus can have over a person's heart. He shows us how it is possible for someone to construct his or her whole universe around Jesus. John succeeds in making us perceive "the unique fullness, the unimaginable wonder of the person of Jesus."[9]

Let us reflect for a moment. After having presented the divine *Logos* in his transcendence and universality, the Gospel writer goes on to say that this *Logos* was concretely made flesh, as a baby. Not only that, but this Gospel presents a *Logos* who eats, drinks, sleeps, gets tired and finally is crucified. To get an idea of the reaction this provoked in learned people of that time, we only need to consider the reasoning of the pagan philosopher Celso: How could this be the Logos, the Son of God? A man who was "shamefully bound and disgracefully punished?"[10] How can this man, who was born in an obscure village in Judea of a poor mother who was a spinner and who began to teach not long ago, be the so-called Son of God?[11]

John's Gospel is on a complete collision course here with ancient thought, as it is with modern thinking. God became a human being without ceasing to be God; the universal became the particular without ceasing to be the universal! It is the greatest of all stumbling blocks and calls for a leap of faith. John overcame it in a single bound and invites us to follow behind him.

Someone has said that the greatest challenge for evangelism in the coming years will be the emergence of a new kind of human being and culture: the cosmopolitan person who moves in a global system of trade and information—from Hong Kong to New York to Rome to Stockholm—that cancels out distance and makes the traditional distinctions of culture and religion recede into the background.

John lived in a cultural context that had something in common with our own. Back then society was experiencing a kind of cosmopolitanism for the first time. The very word *cosmopolitan*—"citizen of the world"—was coined at that time. In the great Hellenistic cities there was an atmosphere of universality and tolerance. It seems that the Emperor Hadrian and then Severus Alexander were disposed to dedicate a temple to Christ too and to give him a place "among the gods."[12] Well then, how did the author of the fourth Gospel react to such a situation? Did he seek to adapt Jesus to a climate in which all religions and cults could find a place and thus to have him accepted as part of a larger whole? Not at all!

John is a great inspiration for us on this issue because he prods us to wager everything on Christ, to be disposed to lose face and to be chased from the synagogue (see John 16:2). The most acute problem during these years after the Council is

Christological, not ecclesial, and we can only hope we realize it before it is too late.

JOHN'S SECRET

John also has a little secret to share with us on this point. How did he arrive at such a total admiration and such an absolute idea of the person of Jesus? How do we explain that his love for Jesus, instead of weakening as time passed, was always increasing?

I believe that, aside from the Holy Spirit, it is due to the fact that he had Jesus' mother close to him. He lived with her, prayed with her and spoke with her about Jesus. It is striking to think that when he composed the phrase "And the Word became flesh," the Gospel writer had nearby, under his own roof, the one in whose womb that mystery was accomplished. Origen wrote, "The first-fruits of the Gospels is [the one] according to John, whose meaning no one can understand who has not leaned on Jesus' breast nor received Mary from Jesus to be his mother also."[13]

Mary communicated her own love for Jesus to this disciple. We need to ask Mary, making use of the communion of the saints, to give us some of her maternal love for Christ. We need exactly this, in fact, a maternal love for Jesus that also serves as a corrective for an excess of theologizing about him. (Taking an interest in Christology does not always mean taking an interest in Christ!) Maternal love is wholly tender, spontaneous and honest; it has no ulterior motives. It is not cerebral but visceral, in the noblest sense of the word. It is a unique love and not even that of the great doctors and mystics can equal it. The icons called "The Mother of Tenderness" try to express this maternal quality of

Mary's love for Jesus. Mary is cheek to cheek with Jesus who has his small hand around her neck.

Jesus is born "through the Holy Spirit of the Virgin Mary." The Holy Spirit and Mary, in different ways, are the two best allies in our effort to draw near to Jesus, to give birth to him in our lives.

Therefore, we ask this of her:

Mother of God, teach us to love Jesus.

Help us to receive him as you received him on that day with infinite adoration, humility, respect, gratitude, love and feeling!

Help us to proclaim and to hear, as if for the very first time, the ancient words ever new: "In the beginning was the Word.... And the Word was made flesh.... We have seen his glory!"

CHAPTER 5

THE WORD BECAME FLESH

A Contemplation of Christ in His Divinity

Saint Paul wrote that when we contemplate Christ, we "are being transformed into the same image from one degree of glory to another; for this comes from the Lord, the Spirit" (2 Corinthians 3:18). The same process occurs in photography: An image is imprinted when it is exposed to the light. A person truly does become what he or she contemplates.

But our contemplation of Christ, I repeat, does not begin and end with us. No one is forced to go the whole way alone. There is a "place" where the fruit of centuries of contemplation of Christ has been gathered: Tradition. We are joining ourselves to that stream of contemplation in that grand "contemplative order," the Church itself. The pattern of "handing on what has been contemplated to others" *(contemplata aliis tradere)* occurs not only on a personal level, in the sense that someone hands on to others what he or she has previously contemplated, but also on a more universal level, in the sense that every generation hands on to succeeding ones and to every branch of Christianity what it has drawn from its own contemplation of Christ.

Let us climb our spiritual Tabor again to spend time contemplating Christ at the school of the great contemplators of the past.

Two "Schools" on Christ

The contemplation of Christ already began, as we saw, with the Synoptic Gospels. It entered into a new phase with the writings of Paul and John. With them, as we saw, two "paths" are marked out, two roads to the discovery of who Jesus Christ is. Paul's path goes from his humanity to his divinity, from the flesh to the Spirit, from the history of Christ to the preexistence of Christ. John's path follows an inverse order and goes from the divinity of the Word to his humanity, from his existence in eternity to his existence in time. Paul places the turning point between the two phases in the *Resurrection* of Christ, and John sees the transition from one status to the other in the *Incarnation*.

In the following era each of the two *paths* tended to solidify, leading to two models or archetypes and finally to two Christological *schools*. None of the followers of either path consciously chooses between Paul and John; everyone is sure of having them both. And that is certainly true. The point is, however, that the two currents remain very visible and distinct, like two rivers flowing together that continue to be distinct because of the different color of their waters.

The difference between the two schools is not so great that some can be said to follow Paul and others John; rather some interpret John in the light of Paul, and others Paul in light of John. The difference is in the pattern or in the underlying perspective that is chosen to illustrate the mystery of Christ.

The two schools I refer to are the Alexandrian school, named for its major center in Alexandria, Egypt, and the Antiochene school, named after the city of Antioch in Syria. In comparing these two schools one can say that they shaped the fundamental outlines of the Church's dogma and theology, which are still operative today. These two schools are responsible in large part, as we will see, for the two complementary but distinct images that have marked Orthodox and Western spirituality, respectively.

These two Christologies assumed their definite form in the period beginning with the Council of Nicea in 325 and ending with the Council of Chalcedon in 451. This is the golden age of the Church's history, a period unequalled for its creativity and the simultaneous presence of so many exceptional men: in the East, Athanasius, Basil, the two Gregories and Cyril; in the West, Ambrose, Augustine and Leo the Great. Leaning on them is like climbing on the shoulders of giants and being able to see an immensely larger horizon.

Today the writings of the Fathers are more like *topics of study* for us, although they were intended primarily as *nourishment*. The difference between the two perspectives would be the same as thoroughly studying a musical score versus enjoying an actual performance of that music. Any time period is impoverished if it detaches itself from the Fathers and thinks it can do just as well on its own—for example, in the interpretation of Scripture—or if it always wants to start over from the beginning, focusing on the epistles of the New Testament while ignoring the paths that others have already laboriously cleared and marked out! People would doom themselves to dealing with the same pitfalls and repeating the same errors that have already been corrected with immense labor and blocking access for themselves to levels of profundity the Fathers already attained.

Therefore the goal of this and of the next meditation is simple: To trace a basic outline of the two "paths" or Christological models, pausing after each one to consider how each can nourish our faith today, make our gospel proclamation more pertinent and rekindle our enthusiasm and love for Christ.

Generally, when people study these topics and the historical period they belong to, they pay the most attention to personality clashes and to the heresies—Apollinarianism and Eutychianism on one hand, and Adoptionism or so-called Nestorianism on the other—that obscure each of the two paths, or to the conduct of some of the protagonists that was not always edifying. It is true that this "golden age" is also one that has left us some of the worst pages in the history of the Church in which ecclesiastical politics, the defense of the supremacy of each one's church (which did not exclude open recourse to corruption) were inextricably mixed with the defense of orthodoxy.

But "God writes straight with crooked lines," and I want to lay aside the "crooked lines" of the human agents and go straight to the positive result willed by God and accepted by the Church. Let us, therefore, prescind completely from the negative and the incidental and seek instead to understand each school's fundamental insight, the perennial contribution that each has added to our understanding of Christ.

CHRIST IN THE ALEXANDRIAN SCHOOL

Of the two paths outlined by Paul and John, John's was the first to be taken up and used. Because of his use of the term *logos*, it offered the ideal instrument for a dialogue with the culture of the time and for combating heresy, especially Arianism. Let us focus on the period of its development, which had its epicenter in Alexandria, in Egypt, precisely during the period between Saint Athanasius and Saint Cyril. First with Athanasius and then with Cyril, we can contemplate this Christological model in its most mature form before and after the crisis that occurred because of the heresy of Apollinarus of Laodicea.

Athanasius' starting point, as we would expect, is John 1:14: "And the Word became flesh." He interprets that statement to mean that "the *Logos* has *become* man, and not merely that he *entered* into a man." The Incarnation does not, then, destroy the Word's transcendence, because "He did not become other than himself on taking the flesh, but, being the same as before, He was robed in it."[1] While he is found in human form, the Word continues to exercise his sovereignty over the universe just as he did before. He is within and outside of all things at the same time.[2]

In the Incarnation the *Logos* takes on flesh and fashions a body for himself in the Virgin's womb that he uses as his "instrument."[3] It is a question therefore of an "incarnation" in the narrowest sense of the word, of the Word's "being made" flesh without, however, any change to himself.

The *unity of Christ* is a given here from the start. Athanasius abhors any descriptions of Christ that separate the Word from the man Jesus. How can people call themselves Christians, he exclaims, who say that the Word has *entered* into a holy man exactly as he used to enter the prophets, instead of saying that he *became* man? How can those people assert that the man is Christ but the Word is *Logos*?

The fundamental insight of this school is clear here and became the supporting plank of all the Church's Christology:

Christ is one single person who is the eternal Word. The language was not yet so well defined, but the idea was perfectly defined.

The *Logos* is thus for Athanasius the dominant principle in Jesus Christ, the unique subject referred to in what is said about him in all the experiences and actions described in the Gospels. The same identical Word performed miracles and yet wept, was hungry, did not know the date of the parousia, prayed in Gethsemane and cried out from the cross.[4]

It could seem difficult to reconcile such different experiences in one same person—that was the Arian argument—but Athanasius traces a careful distinction between the experiences that belonged to the Word *in his eternal being* and those that belonged to him *insofar as he was incarnate.* His explanation for Christ's limitations or sufferings is that they were not *real* but *pedagogical.* If the Scripture said that Jesus grew in wisdom and grace, it meant that there was a connection between his physical development and the *manifestation* of his wisdom. As *Logos,* he knew everything, but having become flesh, which is by nature ignorant, it was fitting that he *seemed* to be ignorant.[5]

This is the how the concept of Christ as a divine subject who enters into history and takes on human flesh, without creating any duality or splitting of himself, was firmly established in Christian consciousness. However, a serious gap—Christ's limitations were not real but pedagogical—prevented this vision from being easily accepted by all Christians. It will be a disciple and friend of Athanasius, Apollinarus, Bishop of Laodicea, who will expose and widen this gap, explaining and theorizing about it. We can summarize his thinking and that of his followers this way: Christ has a human body, but not a human soul; the soul, understood in the highest sense of intelligence and will, is substituted by the Word who performs those functions himself. If in fact the soul is nothing more than "a spark of the *Logos*," there is obviously no need for a *part* when the *whole* is already present. Furthermore, the presence of a free will in Christ would compromise his sinlessness and thus our salvation.

With these premises there is no way to find an adequate explanation for facts like Christ's suffering and lack of knowledge. Without a human soul in Christ to which these limitations could be attributed, there was nothing left but to deny them in order to avoid attributing them to the Word himself, as the Arians did, which resulted in compromising Christ's full divinity and immutability.

This gap was closed by Saint Cyril of Alexandria who developed this vision of Christ to its completion. In his case, more than any other, we need to prescind from the ways and means he uses to affirm his doctrinal position and to concentrate only on the doctrine.

In the wake of Athanasius, he too did not distinguish two *natures* in Christ, God and man, but only two *phases* of a unique existence: first without flesh, then with flesh; one before the Incarnation and one after it. The Incarnation becomes the fundamental turning point or the great divide. The *Logos*—Cyril likes to say—remains who he was: "Immutable by nature, he remains that which he was and is for ever."[6]

What happens in the Incarnation is that, continuing to be in the form of God, he assumes the form of a servant.[7] For Cyril it was not the case that two forms or two natures became united, but that one person united within himself two forms, two modes of existence. He will never quite say "two natures" except at the end, and with reservation, but he will use the famous formula

"*One Incarnate Nature of God the Word.*"[8] (Following the Council of Chalcedon, the refusal to abandon Cyril's formula led to the formation of the Eastern Monophysite Church. Only in 1990, with the common declaration of Chambésy,[9] did it return to communion with the Orthodox Chalcedonian Church, when the two Churches recognized that their disagreement was over terminology rather than doctrine.)

Cyril's contribution to the perfecting of the Athanasian Christological model is twofold. On one hand, he overcame the pitfall of Apollinarianism by recognizing in Christ a *full humanity* equipped not only with a body but also with a rational soul. On the other hand, he introduced the definitive category that explains the union of the two realities of Christ, the *hypostatic union*.[10] The hypostatic union is more than a "conjunction" based on the harmony of Christ's two wills—human and divine. It goes beyond any extraneous and artificial explanation of the unity in Christ and places it on the level of his person or *hypostasis*, that is, on the deepest and most intimate level that one can imagine. It is a union for which human experience offers no other example. It is precisely for this reason that Christ is unique, absolutely different in his inner constitution from all the saints and prophets.

In this vision, the body of Christ is the body "of God" not of a man,[11] with absolutely no confusion or mixture or absorption of one by the other between Christ's humanity and his divinity.

If the Incarnation, understood in its full significance together with doctrine of the Trinity, is the specific characteristic of Christianity that distinguishes it from every other religion, we can say that this "specific" characteristic was established, now for the first time, in all its force and placed at the very center of the edifice of faith. Everything else flows logically from this, and first of all the vigorous defense of the title *Theotokos* given to Mary: She is the true Mother of God because the person who was born of her is one single person who is divine.

This is the highest exaltation of Christianity as a religion of grace: the descent of God toward human beings, rather than the ascent of human beings toward God. In this vision Christ appears more as a *gift* of God that we should receive with awe and gratitude than as a *model* to imitate in life. He is Emmanuel, literally "God with us."

To understand the spiritual fruitfulness of this image of Christ, we should remember one thing in particular: While remaining distinct, each of the two realities of Christ participates in the prerogatives of the other. Thus, if the Word shares the humiliation and suffering of the flesh, which becomes the "suffering of God," then Christ's flesh shares in the divine energy and glory of the Word and becomes "life-giving" through its union with the life of the Word. The consequences of this principle on the spiritual and salvific level will become clear when we go on to consider the Eucharist. Contact with the flesh of Christ becomes contact with the Word himself and with his divine life.

However, before going on to illustrate the consequences of this vision on the spiritual level, it is worthwhile to point out that this vision of Christ is not archaic or irrelevant to current problems in the Church. On the contrary, it is more than ever useful and necessary today. In the encyclical *Redemptoris Missio*, we read, among other things, that "to introduce any sort of separation between the Word and Jesus Christ is contrary to Christian faith."[12] This is a response to theories that make use of a presumed "revealed surplus of the *Logos* with respect to

Christ" to conclude that it is not absolutely necessary for other religions to have an orientation to Christ the Incarnate Word—even if he is implicit and "anonymous" there. It is only necessary to have an orientation to the eternal and timeless *Logos* to whom all religions, in different ways, are individually connected.

This viewpoint removes any rationale for the mission to all peoples and consequently to Christ's explicit command to go make disciples of "all the nations" (Matthew 28:19). The Christology that I have outlined so far contains the clearest response and the firmest no to this separation between the eternal *Logos* and the historical Christ.

MADE ALIVE BY THE SPIRIT OF CHRIST

Now let us look at how these same authors, Athanasius and Cyril, developed a coherent doctrine of salvation and sanctification from this vision of Christ outlined so far, which profoundly influenced later spirituality, especially Orthodox spirituality.

Athanasius never tires of repeating the principle that the Word assumed humanity so that we might become divinized.[13] If through creation we are "creatures" of God, it is only thanks to the Incarnation that we have also become "children" of God. In becoming a human being, Christ made us children of the Father. As the Word, the very principle of life, he overcame death through his coming, and the gift of incorruptibility entered the world.[14] By the simple fact that the Word became flesh, life entered into the world. In a certain sense, by assuming human flesh, he assumed and gave life to all human flesh, humanity still being understood in Plato's wake as a kind of single universal nature. Gregory of Nazianzus will say that when Christ became incarnate, man became God, since he is united to God.[15] With

Christ, in a real sense, God entered into the world and the world entered into God.

However, the divinization does not happen through the sharing of *nature* but through the sharing of the *Spirit*. It is the Holy Spirit who transforms us from simple creatures into children: "But this is God's kindness to men, that of whom he is Maker, of them according to grace He afterwards becomes Father also; becomes, that is, when men, His creatures, receive into their hearts, as the Apostle says, 'the Spirit of His Son, crying Abba, Father.'"[16]

The Holy Spirit is at the center, or at the conclusion, of this vision of Christ. The divine life communicated by the incarnated Word is none other than the Holy Spirit, which is his own Spirit.

If we go from Christology to soteriology (from who Christ is to what he does), the Incarnation, as we can see, remains the starting point and the focal point of everything. It functions not only to explain the *person* of Christ but also the *salvation* he brought. The challenge here, if anything, is to succeed in equally appreciating the *paschal mystery* of the death and resurrection of Christ and to find more than a marginal place for it in the plan of salvation. If in fact all we needed came simply through the Incarnation, whereby we became children and received the Spirit of Christ, what would be the point of Christ's death and resurrection?

Athanasius made some clear progress on this, even if it was still not definitive. He saw the sacrifice of Christ on the cross as necessary for a *full* salvation: In addition to the *restoration of the image of God* that had already come through the Incarnation, the *cancellation of the debt* that man had contracted with God because of sin was also necessary. The death of Christ was the necessary expiation for the sins of human beings.[17] This is more than simply "vicarious substitution"; because of the intimate union between his flesh and ours, "the death of all was consummated in the Lord's body."[18] The foundation here is real and ontological, not juridical.

This attempt to integrate the paschal mystery into a vision focused on the Incarnation was taken up and completed by Cyril. It is precisely the Incarnation that establishes the proper value of the paschal mystery by showing "who" the person is who suffers and dies.

However, what is of most interest is how Cyril carried this vision to its definitive form—a vision in which salvation consists in the *life-giving and deifying contact of the Word with human nature* realized through the Incarnation. He writes, "The goal of the Incarnation was that the Word, the giver of life, taking on human nature in its corruption and decadence, would make it incorruptible, just as fire transfers its heat to iron when they come into contact."[19]

The authors of this school have sometimes been accused by Protestant authors of conceiving of salvation "almost as a chemical process." But in reality, it is not a physical or natural osmosis that occurs between divinity and humanity but a spiritual one. For Saint Cyril as well, the Holy Spirit is the key to understanding everything. The life that the Word communicates is his own Spirit. The fundamental action of the Spirit is precisely to communicate to us the very life of the Word, to make us "participants in the divine nature" (2 Peter 1:4). "The Spirit conforms us to Christ by conferring holiness on us. The Spirit of Christ, in fact, is like a form that he imprints on us, like a divine configuration imprinting itself."[20]

The Spirit does not imprint the image of God in us the way a painter would; he does it by imprinting his very self. He gives us not only *"adiuvante"* ("helping") grace but also participation in the divine nature. It is through the Holy Spirit that we are divinized. The doctrine of "uncreated" grace[21] finds its full affirmation here.

We can note here as well that these ideas retain all their power and relevance today. We live in an age that has been defined by an "awakening in the Spirit." The twentieth century has been marked by the birth and amazing development of Pentecostal churches and the charismatic renewal. New attention to the Holy Spirit is reported in all the sectors of the Church's life: liturgy, theology, piety and evangelization.

What can the vision I have just outlined tell us today that would be useful? There is one essential thing that is often over-looked: The fundamental action of the Holy Spirit does not express itself primarily in the flowering of charisms, the renewal of institutions, or the conferring of power to evangelize. This is all, in a certain sense, "secondary," that is, it comes secondly or afterward. The first and primary thing is the sanctifying action of the Spirit: His communication of the very life and power of the incarnated Word to Christians, his making us "conformed" to Christ by living through the very life of Christ. Without this, everything else is superficial and, to a great extent, unfruitful. The new Pentecost cannot be limited to renewing the exterior of the Church; it must renew the heart of every baptized person. This is a very timely and providential reminder not to quench the ardor of those who are enthusiastic about the Spirit but to give them a solid and deep foundation!

Another contribution of this classical theology is its *ecumenical character*. It stimulates Protestant theology to go beyond its original conception of justification as an extrinsic and forensic imputation. The principle "just and at the same time sinner" *(simul iustus et peccator)* finds its most efficacious corrective in this vision. Conversely, the Protestant Lutheran vision can fulfill an analogous task of balancing this objective "Greek" vision based on a divinization that could lead, if not correctly understood, to a devaluation of the importance of faith and give the impression of a salvation that is almost "by a chemical process" or by simple "grafting."

In the dialogue with other religions, Alexandrian Christology, which seems so exclusive, is instead something that opens up vaster horizons, at least for us Christians, and makes us more optimistic about the salvation of those who live outside the Church. Through it, in fact, the simple presence of the Word in the world, thanks to the Incarnation, reaches down in some way and redeems all of humanity at its very depths, regardless of religious differences, because of the solidarity of the human race. The basis for affirming this solidarity is, of course, no longer the Platonic idea noted above. The basis is that there is one single Creator, one single Spirit who moves in all the Earth, one single human destiny. But the significance of this solidarity remains and is stronger today than it was in the past. In that respect, the year 2000 was a date that concerned not only Christians—it was for the whole human race.

"WHOEVER EATS ME WILL LIVE BECAUSE OF ME": THE EUCHARIST

The image of Christ and of salvation elaborated in John's wake finds its fulfillment, thanks especially to Cyril, on the sacramental level in a concept of the Eucharist that is still wholly valid today. This is where all the effort of dogmatic clarification concerning Christ brings forth its loveliest fruit. After so many centuries we can still find the opportunity to renew our experience of Communion through this eucharistic doctrine.

Several texts will help us enter into the heart of this doctrine. From the outset it is clear that it is depends on a particular way of understanding the Incarnation and is its corollary:

> "And the Word became flesh." He [John] was not content to claim that...[Christ] came to be *in* the flesh but went so far as to say that he *became* flesh, in order to represent the union.... Therefore he who eats the holy flesh of Christ has eternal life. For the flesh contains the Word who is by nature Life.[22]

The Eucharist is a seed of immortality sown in people that in the end will make them rise from the dead. Cyril's text continues,

> If Christ comes to be in us through his own flesh, we shall certainly rise. For it is not credible, or rather, it is impossible that he should not endow with life those in whom he comes to dwell. It is as if one took a glowing ember and thrust it into a large pile of straw in order to preserve the vital nucleus of the fire. In the same way our Lord Jesus Christ hides away life within us by means of his own flesh, and inserts immortality into us, like some vital nucleus that destroys every trace of corruption in us.[23]

As we await the final resurrection, the Eucharist even now exercises a *power to heal* in whoever receives it:

> Partake of the Eucharist in the conviction that it dispels not only death but even the diseases that are in us (cf. 1 Cor. 11:30). For when Christ has come to be within us he lulls to sleep the law that rages in the members of the flesh. He rekindles our reverence towards God, while simultaneously causing the passions to atrophy. He does not reckon our faults against us. Instead, he tends us as a doctor would his patients.[24]

Everything here is extremely concrete and realistic. Whoever eats Christ's body and drinks his blood becomes "one with him, mixed and mingled with him…[just as] if someone were to fuse together two pieces of wax."[25] Just as leaven leavens the whole lump, so too a small portion of eucharistic bread fills our whole bodies with divine energy. He is in us and we are in him, just as the leaven is in the dough and the dough is in the leaven. Thanks to the Eucharist, we become "con-corporeal" with Christ.[26] Only when we read Jesus' words with these premises can we fully appreciate their profundity: "Just as…I live because of the Father, so whoever eats me will live because of me" (John 6:57). These words will become the classic text for this understanding of the Eucharist.[27]

The practical implication of all this is a pressing exhortation to frequent Communion, a point for which Saint Cyril's authority was often invoked later on against the Jansenists. Some people, he notes, cite Paul that whoever eats unworthily is "answerable for the body and blood of the Lord" (1 Corinthians 11:27), but the conclusion to take from this passage is not to abstain from frequent Communion but to purify ourselves as quickly as possible so that we can approach it. In fact, how can you ever become worthy if not by drawing near to the holiness of Christ?[28]

There is, I repeat, complete consistency between this understanding of the Eucharist and the idea these authors held about the Incarnation. Just as in the Incarnation the Word, entering into the flesh assumed from Mary, communicates his divinity to that flesh and through it infuses all of humanity with his divine life and incorruptibility, so too in Communion the Word, entering into a baptized person, infuses him or her with the Spirit and life.

Again, just as in the Incarnation the Word draws flesh to himself, although leaving it in tact with all its properties, that is, without mixture or change, so too in Communion Christ draws human beings to himself and confers on them his mode of being. The most powerful principle of life, in fact, is that the stronger assimilates the weaker, not vice versa. The vegetable assimilates the mineral, not vice versa; the animal assimilates the vegetable and the mineral, not vice versa. So too, now on a spiritual plane, it is the divine that assimilates the human into itself, not vice versa.

However, while in all the other cases the one who eats assimilates whatever it eats, in this case the one who eats is assimilated by the one who is eaten. There is not only *communion* between the two but *assimilation*. Communion is not only the union of two bodies, minds and wills but an assimilation into the one body, the one mind and will of the Word: "Anyone united to the Lord becomes one spirit with him" (1 Corinthians 6:17).

Faith in the real presence of Christ in the Eucharist finds its strongest expression in this tradition. The Eucharist is understood as the sacrament that "prolongs" and makes the Incarnation present.

A person only needs to read *The Life in Christ* by Nicholas Cabasilas to see the extent to which this vision of the Eucharist has shaped the ensuing spirituality of the Orthodox Church. Almost all the themes we have considered are taken up there and woven into a marvelous synthesis of mystical spirituality. In a bold use of the communication of idioms[29] typical of this tradition, the Eucharist is called "God's body."[30] Cabasilas writes:

> Christ infuses himself into us and mingles Himself with us. He changes and transforms us into Himself, as a small drop of water is changed by being poured into an immense sea of ointment. This ointment can do such great things to those who fall into it, that it not only makes us to be sweet-smelling and redolent thereof, but our whole state becomes the sweet-smelling savour of the perfume which was poured out for us.[31]

This eucharistic doctrine can help those who celebrate Mass or take Communion every day not to approach it simply as "praxis"—although this is justified by the infinite value of every Mass or by similar considerations—but rather to approach it as a vital "need" for the soul:

> Yet we are such wretched material that the seal cannot remain unaffected, "for we have this treasure in earthen vessels" (2 Cor 4:7). We therefore partake of the remedy, not once for all, but constantly. The potter must constantly sit by the clay and repeatedly restore the shape which is being blurred. We must continually experience the Physician's hand as He heals the decaying matter and raises up the failing will, lest death creep in unawares.[32]

TRANSFIGURATION IN THE ALEXANDRIAN SCHOOL

We have contemplated Christ through the eyes of an entire school and an important branch of Tradition, but it has not told us everything. The mystery of Christ is not exhausted by an explanation of his Incarnation. Concerning the Eucharist there is much more emphasis on the moment of *communion* than on its *consecration*, more emphasis on its relation to the Incarnation than to the death of Christ, of which we know it is the memorial. We will soon examine the other voice of tradition, the Antiochene school, which took more inspiration from Paul, to round out the whole picture. But what the Alexandrians have told us does not need anything further to be received. It is not the whole truth, but all of it is true.

The Transfiguration is the Gospel scene that best synthesizes the vision of Christ we have contemplated in this meditation, a Christ in whom the overwhelming light and glory of divinity make even the flesh divine and are manifested through it. The following important text of the Byzantine era confirms this, summarizing the essential themes of Tradition outlined so far, especially eucharistic ones, in connection with the Transfiguration of Christ. Gregory Palamas writes:

> Since the Son of God, in his incomparable love for men, did not only unite his divine hypostasis to our nature by putting on an animated body and a soul endowed with intelligence, in order to appear on earth and live among men, but since he also united himself to the human hypostases themselves, in mingling himself with each faithful by communion with his holy body, and since he becomes one body with us…and makes a temple of the whole divinity—for in the very body of Christ *dwells corporally all the*

fullness of the divinity (Col 2:9)—how should we not illuminate those who worthily communicate with the divine ray of his body which is within us, lightening their soul, as he illumined the very bodies of the disciples on Thabor [*sic*]? For then that body, source of the light of grace, was not yet united to our bodies; it illumined from without those who worthily approached it and sent the illumination to the soul by the intermediary of the eyes of the sense; but today since it is mingled with us and exists in us, it illuminates the soul from within.[33]

We can descend again from our Tabor now, knowing that the Eucharist offers us the daily opportunity for a concrete experience of the wonders of grace that we have in Christ and that the Alexandrian Fathers helped us glimpse. The world, they tell us, has changed since the time the eternal Word of God descended and made it his dwelling. May we all, two thousand years after that coming, become newly aware of this truth!

CHAPTER 6

OBEDIENT UNTO DEATH

A Contemplation of Christ in His Humanity

Let us quickly review the road we have traveled thus far, to see the "base" from which we depart for our new ascent of Mount Tabor. The mystery of the Transfiguration is a kind of ideal "observatory" in which to position ourselves to contemplate that spiritual firmament that is Christ. We have located in Scripture and tradition the great "parabolic reflector" capable of gathering and amplifying the lights that reach us from this firmament.

For the great contemplation of Christ acting in history, I have chosen those important periods that have contributed the most in defining his final image in the Church's consciousness. After the two foundational paths associated with Paul and John, I come now to the period that spans the fourth and fifth centuries, during which the two schools of Alexandria and Antioch reached their peak and prepared the ground for the crystallization of Christological doctrine.

Understanding the soul or the basic insight of each of these two schools is a necessary path to an understanding of the Christ of faith that is more than superficial. After having reviewed the characteristic traits of the Alexandrian Christ, it is now time for me to offer a similar reflection on the Christ of the Antiochene school. The originality of the Alexandrian Christ is not fully understood unless it is compared with the one from the Antiochene school and vice versa.

Let us ascend Tabor, then, to contemplate the Savior through the eyes and the hearts of the Antiochene Fathers. We will see in this chapter how, in some respects, this means going back to the sources of our own Latin vision of Christ. One of the masters of the Antiochene school, Irenaeus, from Asia Minor in Gaul, became one of the founders of western theology.

The term "Antiochene school" signifies a certain approach to theology and biblical exegesis that had its center in Antioch in Syria, the third greatest city of the empire after Rome and Alexandria before the rise of Constantinople. The first bishop at Antioch was Saint Peter and, after him, Saint Ignatius of Antioch. The most notable representatives of this school were the bishops Eustathius of Antioch, Melitius, Diodore of Tarsus, Saint John Chrysostom, Theodore of Mopsuestia and Theodoret of Cyrrhus.

We will encounter here and there a few terms or concepts that could seem difficult and different from our way of speaking today, so let us not get discouraged but keep moving forward. At the end we will see that the important nucleus of their thought will become very clear and open to surprising contemporary applications.

I am also selecting here a few of the most famous representatives, in particular Theodore of Mopsuestia, to reconstruct the orientation of their school. I will also forego discussing here the negative or polemical elements and go straight to this school's positive contribution, which was subsequently incorporated into the Chalcedonian definition.

I am not going to reconstruct, in this setting, the entire thinking of the Antiochene authors, their sources, their errors, their arguments. (There are many other places in which this can be done much better.) These authors interest us only insofar as they help us to discover something new about Jesus Christ. We are not looking at them but in the same direction they did. The Letter to the Hebrews repeatedly admonishes us to "consider...Jesus" (3:1), and fixing our gaze on Jesus is precisely what we will try to do.

A Return to the Christ of the Gospels

The way to understand the Antiochene approach to the mystery of Christ appears clearly in a text from Theodore of Mopsuestia. After quoting the passage from Philippians 2:6–7 on Christ—"though he was in the form of God...[he] emptied himself, taking on the form of a slave"—he comments:

> In saying this he [Paul] made a clear distinction between the natures of the one who is in the form of God and the one who is in the form of a servant.... And he taught us also about the human nature in which our Lord was, as he said congruous things concerning the form of the servant which He assumed: "He humbled Himself and became obedient unto death, even the death of the

Cross. Wherefore God also hath highly exalted Him and given Him a name which is above every name."[1]

The text from Paul that speaks about the two "forms" Christ was clothed in (the form of God and the form of servant) has the same importance for this school that John's text—"And the Word became flesh"—had for the Alexandrians. Paul's text comes up every time these authors want to provide a biblical foundation for their positions.[2] They see this text—and rightly so—as expressing the truths they most desired to assert about Christ: His two realities, divinity and humanity, humility and glory, with the Resurrection as the point of transition from one state to the other. The positive result of this choice is that the gospel is opened again to a holistic reading without the constant need to resort to artificial "pedagogical" explanations about this or that human limitation attributed to Jesus.

> Many things…happened to Him according to human law: things which we may learn from the Gospel. He was wrapped in swaddling clothes after He was born and laid in a manger; He was circumcised after the custom of the law…; He…endured all things dealing with His increase in stature, wisdom and favour, while He was subject unto His parents.[3]

This focus spurred a providential return to contact with the historical Jesus of the Gospels, after more than a century of anti-Arian polemic that had forced them to be exclusively focused on the eternal *Logos*. The path that emerges here is clearly Pauline: It begins with Christ "according to the flesh" and, with the Resurrection, leads to Christ "the Son of God," who lives according to the Spirit.

There were of course some polemical motives at the root of their emphasis: to oppose Arianism by showing how the divinity of the Word is not compromised by Christ's human limitations and to combat Apollinarianism by affirming the full humanity of Christ. But the real reason goes much deeper: The authors of this school were essentially biblical exegetes. For them the philosophical influence of Middle Platonism, although not absent, takes second place in comparison to the attention they pay to biblical categories.

This explains the surprisingly modern, historical character of their reconstruction that lines up, in certain respects, with the results of the contemporary study of the Christology of the New Testament. They are easily able, for example, to acknowledge a *real development* in the life of Christ: "All that which He did for us He did according to the law of our nature, so that He grew little by little, reached full age and performed also carefully the requirements of the law."[4]

As man, Jesus truly grew in wisdom and grace, overcoming temptations and learning obedience until he became perfectly obedient. Only at the end, in his risen state, is his union with God fully revealed. That union, it should be noted, does not depend on his development as a human because it existed from the moment of his conception. It is not a union with the eternal Word that is progressively developed in the life of Christ. Rather, the fact of that union is manifested in various ways and degrees as the humanity he took on—the "assumed man" as the Antiochians called him—grows and develops through the normal course of life and through the interventions of the heavenly Father.[5]

In an observation worthy of modern gospel criticism, Theodore says that the apostles themselves came to discover the divinity of Christ only at the end: "One finds in the Book of the Gospel many passages which demonstrate that the Apostles were not aware of the Divinity of the Only Begotten before the Crucifixion."[6]

This unmistakable progression is tied to the fact that these authors definitively and safely sailed past the reef on which Alexandrian Christology had run aground, that is, the failure to recognize a genuine human soul in Christ. The Antiochians not only acknowledge the existence of such a soul, but they also are able, as we will see, to ultimately assign it an appropriate role in the economy of salvation.

Those who do not recognize a human soul in Jesus, Theodore argues, cannot explain how it can be said that Jesus "grew in age and wisdom." For opposite reasons, in fact, neither the divinity nor the body of Christ by itself alone can grow in wisdom: His divinity does not need it, and his body is not capable of it.[7] There is no longer any need for recourse to handy explanations for his lack of knowledge of the parousia, the agony at Gethsemane and the other experiences of Jesus on Earth that had caused so much embarrassment during the polemic against Arianism.

The first to benefit from the fruit of this different approach to the problem were really the Alexandrians. Even Saint Cyril of Alexandria, spurred on by this solution, begins to admit, little by little, that the human soul is the principle of the Redeemer's suffering and that it plays a decisive role in his obedience and his offering of himself on the cross.[8] This new way of reading the Gospels, made normative by the Antiochians, appears in the poetic text of a faithful disciple of that school, Narsai, who lived in the second half of the fifth century:

> He was laid in a manger and wrapped in swaddling clothes, as Man; and the watchers extolled Him with their praises, as God.... He kept the Law completely, as Man; and He gave His own new law, as God; He was baptized in the Jordan by John, as Man; and the heaven opened in honour of His baptism, as God. He went in to the marriage-feast of the city of Cana, as Man; and He changed the water that it became wine, as God. He fasted in the wilderness forty days, as Man; and watchers descended to minister unto Him, as God.... He ate and drank and walked and was weary, as Man; and He put devils to flight by the word of His mouth, as God.... He asked water of the Samaritan woman, as Man; and he revealed and declared her secrets, as God. He sat at meat in the Pharisee's house, as Man; and He forgave the sinful woman her sins, as God. He went up into the mountain of Tabor with His disciples, as Man; and He revealed His glory to their sight, as God.... He prayed and sweated at the time of His passion, as Man; and He scared and terrified them that took Him, as God.... He was hanged upon the wood and endured the passion as Man; and he shook the earth and darkened the sun, as God.... He cried out upon the cross, "My God, My God," as Man; and He promised Paradise to the thief, as God.... They embalmed His body and He was buried in the earth, as Man; and He raised up His temple by His mighty power, as God.[9]

THE UNITY OF CHRIST

But what about the unity of Christ at this point? Harmonizing the two aspects of Christ (God and man) with his unity highlights the limitation of this school. It is not a question of heresy, at least not in the phase we are considering, but rather of a lack of conceptual tools to resolve the problem. The dogma was in the process of being formulated, so these authors reflected the doctrine in its "nascent state" before it was "defined."

It is not the case that these authors deny the union of divinity and humanity in Christ, which, on the contrary, was required by the very concept of salvation that they were developing. It was only that they lacked the means to express it. This means had been found in Alexandria in the concept of the "hypostatic union," a personal union or a union in the person. However, this concept was unacceptable to the Antiochians because its inventor, Apollinarius of Laodicea, had used it to exclude the soul of Christ, which resulted in making the concept incompatible with his full humanity. *Hypostasis* continued to mean for them—like the equivalent *sub-stantia* for the Latin writers—not what is one in Christ but what is twofold in him.

The same difficulty arises, but in reverse, for the Alexandrians. The Antiochians found the means to affirm the full humanity of Christ and the distinction between divinity and humanity through the concept of the distinction between *natures (physis)*. But this concept seemed unacceptable to the Alexandrians because that term—in its older use—indicated for them what was one in Christ and not what was twofold. They were lacking a term to express the duality, just as the Antiochians were lacking a term to express the unity.

The distinction between nature and person, in other words, the birth of the metaphysics of personhood, unknown in Antiochene thinking, seems to have been the most arduous undertaking in Christian thinking to bring to a conclusion. Most of the difficulties and the confrontations between Latins and Greeks, and among the Greeks themselves, in the articulation of Trinitarian and Christological doctrine stem from this. If there was a sin in all these conflicts, it was the sin of impatience.

But let us try to understand how the unity of the person of Christ was conceived of in the Antiochene vision of Christ. Theodore openly rejects the doctrine that the man Jesus and the Word constitute "two distinct Sons of God," one natural and one adopted. He never tires of repeating that the distinction of the natures does not impede their unity:

> Let us learn the distinction between natures.... [However,] we should also be mindful of that inseparable union through which that form of man can never and under no circumstances be separated from the Divine nature which put it on. The distinction between the natures does not annul the close union nor does the close union destroy the distinction between the natures.[10]

The union between the assumed humanity and the Word who assumes it is explained by the idea of *inhabitation*, suggested by the fact that Jesus once called his body a "temple" (see John 2:19). For the Antiochians the verse "And the Word became flesh" is interpreted in the light of the words that follow it: "and *lived* among us" (John 1:14). It is a question of a union "according to *bene placito (kat' eudokian)*"—that is, by favor, by grace, by pleasure, by free initiative—but different than what exists in every other case, for example, between God and a prophet or God and a saint. It is different because this union does not come as the result of holy conduct but precedes it; it exists from the very beginning and is indissoluble.

Is it a union that is different in *degree* or also in *nature?* This is the point that was not clarified. Theodore frequently uses the word *person* to designate the unity. But *person (prosopon)* does not have the meaning that *hypostasis* has for the Alexandrians. It is not the preexistent person of the Word who takes on flesh and confers his own personality on it, but it is in a certain sense the result of the union of both—divinity and humanity—even if it is true that the primacy and all the initiative depend on the Word and not on the man. "The natures which are brought together make up one person according to the union."[11] *Person* here means generically one "subject," one individual—a "person" in the way we normally use the term. For Theodore of Mopsuestia, it is a union that is sufficient to justify the communication of idioms[12] that he frequently employed, even if he did so with caution and never with the same ease as the Alexandrians.[13]

THE KIND OF SAVIOR WE NEED

How is it that the Christ contemplated at Antioch has characteristics that are so new and different when compared to the Christ of Alexandria? The reasons are certainly multiple. These authors are heirs to a line of thinking—the so-called Asiatic theology—of whom one of the leading proponents is Irenaeus, who focuses more on the history of salvation than on theological speculation.

A revealing detail emerges in the interpretation given by both sides for the title "image of God" that Saint Paul uses for Christ (see Colossians 1:15). Irenaeus had applied this title to Christ insofar as, through the Incarnation, he became "the visible image of the invisible God." For him the fact that human beings were created "in the image of God" meant that they were created "in the image of the future Christ." Christ in his resurrection is the new Adam, the true and perfect image of God and model of a human being. That explanation, quickly taken up among the Latins by Tertullian, is also common to the Antiochians. Theodore writes, "Every image, while itself seen, points to what is not seen. So it cannot happen that an image be made which is such as not to be seen."[14]

For him then, "the image of God" is Christ insofar as he is a human being. On the other hand, in the Alexandrian school from Origen on, it was thought that the image of the invisible should itself be invisible to accurately represent the thing it depicts. Therefore, the phrase is applied to Christ insofar as he is *Logos*, the Son of God. From whatever vantage point they are considered, these two different centers of interest always emerge: the eternal *Logos* for the Alexandrians, the historical Christ for the Antiochians.

There are, then, long-standing reasons that explain the different orientation operating in the Antiochene school. However, the chief reason is something else. These men, especially Theodore of Mopsuestia, oriented more to biblical exegesis than to philosophical speculation, were removed—if not completely, at least in large part—from the prevailing influence of Middle Platonism and developed a vision of human beings closer in many respects to that of the Bible.

A person is not only or chiefly a metaphysical entity, but a moral reality. A person is "in the image of God" not only because of his or her intelligence that is related to the divine universal reason. A human being is "in the image of God" with all his or her being, soul and body, because only a human body, being visible, can actualize the concept of an image, which is to represent or make something visible. Just as our souls manifest themselves outwardly through our bodies, so too it is through the entire human being—body and soul—that there is a reflection and an indicator of God. A human being is an image of God insofar as he or she—constituted as sovereign over creation—governs creation in obedience to the will of the Creator. "God created humankind in his image" is read in the light of "Fill the earth and subdue it; have dominion over [it]" (Genesis 1:27–28). If someone stops being obedient, he or she ceases being the image of God or at least ceases *functioning* as an image of God because it is through obedience that a human being is that image.

The function of human reason is not essentially theoretical and contemplative, as in Neoplatonism, but practical. Reason is what allows people to distinguish between good and evil and makes them able to choose good and reject evil. The difference between rational human beings and irrational beings consists precisely in this. Irrational creatures are not able to distinguish good and evil, but reasoning beings are. "They are able to distinguish good from evil and also they choose…what seems best by the power of the will. Further, for them the promulgation of the law is altogether appropriate, since they can learn from it what is good."[15]

What then is the nature of sin if a human being is conceived of in this way? It would not simply be *ignorance*, as it was for the Greeks from Socrates on, but it would be an *evil intention* in a mistaken choice. For the Alexandrians whose thinking was much more shaped by Neoplatonic categories, real sin does not reside in the soul, the intellect or the will, which are related to God and participate in incorruptibility, but resides in the flesh, which is subject to the attraction of material things and pleasures. To save human beings conceived of this way, it was enough to liberate and divinize the flesh so as to prevent the clouding of the mind that then leads to sin.

But to save human beings as conceived of in Antioch, this is not enough. Here sin is seen quite differently. It is above all *disobedience* to God, a voluntary act of rebellion and not simply ignorance. It is rooted in the depths of the soul, more so than in the flesh, even if the flesh, with its passions and lusts, helps lead to sin. Salvation, then, requires that the Savior take on not only flesh to divinize it but also a soul and a will with which to accomplish an act of obedience that would redeem all human disobedience. There is, then, a vital link between anthropology, soteriology and Christology. A human being, understood in biblical terms, requires a certain kind of salvation; in turn, salvation conceived of in this way requires a certain kind of savior.

In light of these two premises, it is not surprising that these authors were so concerned about the full humanity of Christ. If Christ is to save us, he needs to be constituted in such a way that he can accomplish an act of absolute obedience that would inaugurate a new world order characterized by immortality and participation in the life of God. But only if Jesus is truly and perfectly human will he be able to accomplish that task. The concept of obedience involves someone who obeys and someone who is obeyed. God cannot obey himself. Theodore writes:

> If the soul had only sinned in those things that befall it from the passions of the body, it would perhaps have been sufficient for our Lord to have assumed only the body in order to deliver (the soul) from sin. Many, however, and of different kinds are the iniquities and sins that are born of the soul. The first (sin) through which it shows its association with Satan is that of pride.... It is with justice,

therefore, that our Lord assumed the soul so that it should be first delivered from sin and be transferred to immutability by the grace of God through which it overcomes the passions of the body.[16]

Saint Gregory of Nazianzus had already declared that "what was not assumed, was not healed,"[17] and so if the Savior did not take on a soul, the soul is not saved. But the Antiochians went a step further. It is not enough for them that a human soul be passively *assumed* by the Word so that people's souls could be healed. That human soul would need to play an active role rather than merely being something to which everything in Christ that would be "unworthy of God" could be attributed. Christ's humanity cannot simply be the *locus of attribution*, it also needs to be a free and voluntary *principle of action*. Without the principle of humanity of Christ, his salvation would not truly belong to us.

THE PASCHAL MYSTERY

All of this clearly shifts the center of attention from the Incarnation to the paschal mystery. If salvation essentially comes through the free obedience by the new Adam, it is obvious then that the essential event for salvation does not occur at the beginning, in the Incarnation, where his humanity does not yet play an active role, but will occur through the life and, even more, the death and resurrection of Christ.

Only in this framework can the famous Pauline assertions be fully understood and appreciated: "Just as by the one man's disobedience the many were made sinners, so by the one man's obedience the many will be made righteous" (Romans 5:19); "He…became obedient to the point of death—even death on a cross. Therefore God, also highly exalted him" (Philippians

2:8–9); "He learned obedience through what he suffered" (Hebrews 5:8).

Here is how Nestorius, in the wake of Saint Irenaeus, exalts the obedience of the human Christ in a text that still retains all its validity:

> For this [cause] also he took a nature which had sinned, lest in taking a nature which was not subject to sin he should be supposed not to have sinned on account of the nature and not on account of obedience. But, although he had all those things which appertain unto our nature, anger and concupiscence and thoughts, and although also they increased with the progress and increase of every age [of his life], he stood firm in thoughts of obedience.... Nor again in obedience made he use of those [commands of God] wherein there was attraction in honour and power and glory, but of those which in misery and poverty and contempt and weakness could offend the thoughts of obedience.... But for this only was he anxious, to obey God, and he loved that which God willed.[18]

With respect to the paschal mystery, the Antiochians not only emphasized the importance of the death but also of the resurrection of Christ:

> Indeed this resurrection is the end of all the Economy of Christ and the principal object of all the reforms wrought by Him, as it is through it that death was abolished, corruption destroyed, passions extinguished, mutability removed, the inordinate emotions of sin consumed, [and] the power of Satan overthrown.[19]

The Resurrection has not only apologetic value here (to persuade people of the truth about Christ) but also the significance of a mystery. The entire transformation of human nature, which the Alexandrians saw as already accomplished in the moment when the Word took on flesh, is here seen as accomplished in the Resurrection, once again following Paul who had pointed to the Resurrection as the moment in which the new Adam becomes "a life-giving spirit" (1 Corinthians 15:45).

In his paschal mystery Christ did not limit himself to expiating and canceling human disobedience; he did more. On the positive side he inaugurated a new state of affairs, a second age, in which sin is not only forgiven but abolished. We now possess only the first fruits of this "new age" into which Christ entered until we too will enter it through resurrection.

Then is everything fine, everything perfect, from this point of view? No, more than ever the fundamental defect of this school emerges here, that is, its lack of an adequate concept of the personal and hypostatic union in Christ. Precisely in order that the great act of Christ's obedience not be the act of an individual human being that ended with him, but on the contrary initiate a new status for humanity, it was necessary that it be the human act of a God. In order that *grace* be transmitted to make all to become "righteous" and the act not merely be a heroic *example* of obedience, it needed to be a human act of a God. Human, but of a God!

Theodore of Mopsuestia and the other Antiochians aimed at this conclusion with all their might but without succeeding at completely attaining it. Theodore writes, "He Himself [God] was not tried with the trial of death but He was near to him [Christ] and doing the things that were congruous to His nature as the Maker who is the cause of everything."[20]

God is involved in this act of obedience not personally but insofar as he is the cause of everything. It still cannot be said that Christ's obedience is the human obedience of a God. It is the obedience of a man who is forever and indissolubly united to God, but in spite of everything, it is the obedience of a man.

Only when the analysis of Christ's act of obedience is taken up by Maximus the Confessor in the light of Chalcedon will all the strength of the Antiochene insight come forth.[21] It had so far remained unusable because of the defect that accompanied it. In Saint Maximus Christ's obedience appears to be truly the human obedience of a God: "human" by virtue of its quality and "of a God" by virtue of the one to whom it belonged. This is the "rock of our salvation."

THE EUCHARIST, THE MEMORIAL OF THE DEATH AND RESURRECTION OF CHRIST

The Eucharist, for the Antiochians as well, constitutes the sacramental corollary of Christology, the place where its richness appears most clearly and its inadequacy is least noticeable. It was only natural that a concept that highlighted the paschal mystery so strongly would result in a eucharistic doctrine that is particularly rich and evocative. Reading these texts in the light of the clarification brought by Chalcedon, we can freely embrace, without reservation, the treasures of this eucharistic doctrine. The two catecheses by Theodore on the Mass are among the classics of patristic mystagogical catechesis. He writes, "We must first of all realize that we perform a *sacrifice* of which we eat. Although we remember the death of our Lord in food and drink, and although we believe these to be the remembrance of His Passion,…we nevertheless perform…a sacrifice."[22]

From the beginning the Eucharist is clearly presented in its sacrificial aspect. This concept was certainly not unknown to the Alexandrians, but it occupies a more significant position for the Antiochians.

The Eucharist is seen less as the *real presence of a person* than as the *memorial of an event*, the death-resurrection of Christ. In the Alexandrian perspective, eucharistic communion places us in contact with Christ's flesh, which has become life-giving because of the Incarnation and because of its hypostatic union with the Word. In the Antiochene perspective, eucharistic communion puts us in contact above all with Christ's body that gives life because of the Resurrection.

In no other ancient catechesis is the role of the Holy Spirit so accentuated as it is here. The Holy Spirit is not only the one who is *given* to us through the Eucharist but also the one who *gives* us the Eucharist. It is he who comes at the moment of consecration, through the epiclesis, upon the bread and wine and makes them become the Body and Blood of Christ, living and life-giving, just as in the Resurrection he came upon Christ's dead body and raised it to life and immortality:

> Indeed, the body of our Lord, which is from our own nature, was previously mortal by nature, but through the resurrection it moved to an immortal and immutable nature. When the priest, therefore, declares them to be the body and the blood of Christ, he clearly reveals that they have so become by the descent of the Holy Spirit, through whom they have also become immortal, inasmuch as the body of our Lord, after it was anointed and had received the Spirit, was clearly seen so to become. In this same way, after the Holy Spirit has come here also, we believe that the elements

of bread and wine have received a kind of anointing from the grace that comes upon them, and we hold them to be henceforth immortal, incorruptible, impassible, and immutable by nature, as the body of our Lord was after the resurrection.[23]

Everything is centered on the paschal mystery:

Through these remembrances and these signs and symbols which have been performed…all of us draw nigh unto Christ our Lord risen from the dead, with a great joy and happiness. And we joyfully embrace Him with all our power as we see Him risen from the tomb, and we hope also to participate (with Him) in the resurrection.[24]

We draw near to receive the body and blood of Christ with the certainty that through them the divine power of the Resurrection is communicated to us under the form of peace, courage and hope.

In combining the Alexandrian and the Antiochene perspectives, we have a much more complete vision of the Eucharist. It appears to us simultaneously as the real presence of the incarnate Word and as a memorial of his passion and resurrection. It is the sacrament that makes present the mystery of the Incarnation and the paschal mystery at the same time. In both cases the Eucharist is the most faithful mirror of Christology, the place in which all the effort of contemplating Christ, over and above any polemical interest, brings about communion with the one who is contemplated and joyful participation in his mystery.

We can see now what a serious loss it would be for Christian spirituality if only one of these two perspectives—the winning one—should make the other disappear from ongoing discussions in Christian thinking or should confine the other merely to history books. Nevertheless, this is what happened, at least in part, with the Antiochene tradition because of the later condemnation of its representatives—often due to incidental and political reasons—and because of the systematic destruction of their works.

A MODERN GAZE AT CHRIST

The contemplation of Christ that I have tried to set forth in this meditation can be useful in many ways to the Church today, positively and negatively. I will limit myself to noting a few areas.

What strikes us right away about the Antiochene school is the modern character of its approach to Christ. I mean "modern" in the sense of its relevance to the issues that are debated today. To a modern person, much more equipped with a historical sense than with a taste for speculation, the Antiochene Christ, based on constant reference to the Gospels, seems closer and more plausible than the Alexandrian Christ or the Christ of the subsequent Scholastic period who is set forth in terms that are much more metaphysical.

The *concept of a human being* in these authors, at least in the best of them, took on a more biblical and existential character. The human being is no longer seen as a *metaphysical entity*, constituted immutably as such from the beginning, but rather as a *moral reality* destined to form himself or herself, to grow and exercise self-determination though free choices made in obedience to God. A human being is not only what he or she is by birth—a *nature*—but also what he or she is called to become through obedience to God's law—a *vocation*. And we know how close all of this is to a certain trend in modern thought to which we are called to proclaim the gospel today.

Moving on to consider Christ directly, he no longer seems to us only a *gift* descended from heaven to give people life through the sacraments but also a *model* to imitate in life. "And as after He was born of a woman He increased little by little according to the law of humanity, and grew up fully, and was under the law and acted according to it, so also in the life of the Gospel He became an example as man to man."[25]

We can say that here for the first time the theological foundation for the *imitation of Christ* occurs. The Alexandrians also had an ideal of imitation, but for them it was "imitation of God" or "assimilation into God." When they spoke of the imitation of Christ, they meant the imitation of Christ as *Logos*—again, imitation of God. The imitation of Christ's humanity for the Alexandrians is only an inferior stage for beginners, a stage they need to move beyond to attain to the element in him that is divine.

In particular, the focus of the imitation of Christ for the Antiochians was his *obedience*. These authors seem to speak directly to modern people here when they lay bare the true original sin of human beings which is not yielding to the passions of the flesh (this is actually the consequence of sin) but the attempt to make themselves autonomous and independent of God—to act as rulers of the universe but no longer in obedience to the Creator, to become God's adversaries and rivals.

With their insistence on the *voluntary* character of sin, the Antiochians contributed in distinguishing Christianity from paganism and Hellenism in a decisive way. Søren Kierkegaard was unaware of having had such lucid predecessors when he wrote, "Socrates explains that he who does not do what is right has not understood it,...but Christianity goes a little further back and says that it is because he is unwilling to *understand* it, and this again because he does not *will* what is right" (emphasis added).[26]

If, as this philosopher writes, "it is specifically the concept of sin...that most decisively differentiates Christianity qualitatively from paganism,"[27] then the theologians of the Antiochene school brought a noteworthy contribution to its distinction from paganism and the affirmation of the Christian point of view about human beings and sin.

However, we should also note, alongside the merits, a danger that the Antiochene Christology has for us today. It is the tendency to take from it not the positive application that was used at Chalcedon but precisely its negative element, the bitter fruit, which was overcome on that occasion by the Church.

Paul affirms about Christ "according to the flesh" that he "is" God who is over everything (see Romans 9:5). According to Theodore of Mopsuestia the apostle could equally well have said that in Jesus, according to the flesh, God "is present," but Paul did not say it because he held to "the close union between the two natures,"[28] employing the communication of idioms. One can easily intuit that of the two formulations Theodore of Mopsuestia prefers the second.

We know now that resolving the problem of Christ's divinity through the concept of inhabitation (Christ "is" not God, but in Christ God "is present") is seductive and at the foundation of not a few so-called "new Christologies." Christ becomes merely the locus of the supreme revelation of God. Some recent Christologies, in my opinion, have performed a very subtle and insidious operation: They have adopted the Alexandrian *outline* (emphasis on the one person of Christ) but filled it with

Antiochene *content* (clarity about the full humanity of Christ). One of these authors says:

> In Christ…it is primarily not the human nature…but the divine nature in the human person [that is *enhypostatic*[29]].… Our concept could now be called the theory of the *enhypostasia* of the Word. Or, in other words: of the presence of God's Word, or of God through his word, in Jesus Christ.[30]

This is what I would call an Alexandrian outline with Antiochene content: Christ is indeed a single person, but a human, not a divine one. The unity is preserved here but at the expense of divinity. This is not the synthesis made at Chalcedon of the two issues of Christ's unity and his full humanity; this is its reversal.

But while for the Antiochians this issue was a question of a lacuna that still needed to be filled, of a position in the process of being clarified, today it would be a return to a prior stage, a step backward. After the Christological issue was defined at Chalcedon, Nestorius himself, from exile, said he recognized in full the formulation proposed by Pope Leo. He adhered to it, declaring (even if perhaps not completely accurately) that this was what he had always meant.[31] The Antiochians would be the first, then, to refuse this modern solution which compromises not only the unity of the Word and the human being in Christ, but also the very existence of an eternal Word in God and, thus, the Trinity. In this sense the study and the appreciation of the Antiochene image of Christ, far from constituting a danger or a temptation for the theologian today, becomes an incentive not to lose the fruit of so much effort and not to abandon a goal that was achieved with so much difficulty.

Nowadays, fighting for the recognition of the full humanity of Christ—his limitations, experiences and temptations—is like knocking down an open door. Acknowledging his full humanity is what everyone is doing; in fact, there is a kind of competition as to who can push things further in this direction. It was not like this at the time of the Antiochians. At that time, it was truly a victory to restore the full human dimension to Christ. If we want to be faithful and really continue their struggle, we know now what we must highlight the most about Jesus' humanity: his *obedience!* It was to affirm his obedience and its essential contribution to the work of redemption—and not to feel exempt from believing in his divinity—that the Antiochians defended the full humanity of Christ so vigorously.

TWO ROADS TO THE SAME MYSTERY

In these last two meditations, I have tried to outline the Christ of the schools of Alexandria and Antioch that together contributed to the definition of the canonical image of Christ. This definition was brought to completion in Chalcedon and also through the Latin mediation of Pope Leo the Great. It was not a painless operation, demonstrated by the fact that the final settlement was achieved only a few years ago in 1990 with the restoration of communion between the Orthodox Chalcedonian Church and the Eastern Monophysite Church.

How was the agreement of Chalcedon achieved? Through some kind of philosophical or political strategy? No, it was determined that Christ the man-God is, and always will be, a mystery. We can affirm two opposite things about him—divinity and humanity, unity and duality—but how these opposites are reconciled in him will always elude us, and woe to us if we ever believe we have encapsulated him in a concept! We will have misunderstood and diminished him.

What then is the solution for today? We need to travel both roads, one after another, to climb Tabor by the first path and descend by the second and vice versa. Thus we need to follow both the path of humanity and the path of divinity, one after another. This is what we have tried to do, in our own small way, in the reflections up to this point. We climbed Tabor once on Paul's path and once on the path marked out by Saint John, once on the path of divinity of the Alexandrian school, which revealed to us the divine splendors of the *Logos*, and once on the path of humanity of the Antiochene school, which spoke to us of God's humbling himself.

Along with their ideas let us also receive some of their spirit, their inspiring dedication to Christ, which impelled them to give him a place that was so absolute in their thinking and so central in their lives!

CHAPTER 7

THE MEDIATOR

An Image of Christ for the Third Millennium

THE TWO PATHS INTERSECT AT CHALCEDON

It is time for our final ascent of Mount Tabor. We have already seen in the comparison between Saint Paul and Saint John two possible paths marked out for us to approach the mystery of Christ. One path goes from the historical Christ, "according to the flesh," and ends with the Christ declared to be Son of God, "according to the spirit" (Romans 1:3, 4); the other path goes from the eternal *Logos* to the Jesus of history. These two paths become further defined in the two chief Christological schools of antiquity, Alexandria and Antioch. The first emphasizes the divinity of Christ and his unity of person, while the second emphasizes his perfect humanity and the distinction between his two natures.

The synthesis of these two lines of thought occurred, as we know, in the ecumenical Council of Chalcedon in 451, with Saint Leo the Great representing the contribution of the West. There the fundamental truth about the unity of the person of Christ, which had been developed at Alexandria and legitimized by the Council of Ephesus, was combined with the Antiochene insistence on the intact human nature of Christ. The two traditional paths were therefore both recognized as valid, provided that they remained open to and connected with each other.

The way the definition was formulated at Chalcedon embodies this principle. The same mystery of Christ was in fact formulated there twice in different ways. First, moving from the affirmation of unity to the affirmation of the distinction: "The same Lord Jesus Christ, the only-begotten Son, must be acknowledged in two natures."[1] Second, moving from the distinction of natures to the affirmation of unity: "The character proper of each of the two natures was preserved as they came together in one person *(prosopon)* and one hypostasis."[2]

It took two centuries before the situation stabilized and this conclusion was peacefully accepted by the whole Church. The Chalcedonian formulation led to the separation of two groups on the edges of the conflict, birthing the Nestorian Church and the Monophysite Church. The first group separated because they never accepted the condemnation of Nestorius (unjust, in their opinion) and the failure to have him reinstated. The second group separated because they would not accept the abandonment of the rigid Cyrillic formula of "one nature." In both cases it is now commonly believed that the "heresy" at that time—whether Nestorian or Monophysite—consisted more in terminology than in doctrine.

Within the larger Church there would also be two crises before a definitive establishment of the Christological doctrine was achieved. At the Second Council of Constantinople in 553, there was an attempt to tip the balance of the Chalcedonian definition toward the Alexandrian and Cyrillic emphasis on unity by readmitting as legitimate the formula of the "one incarnate nature...of God the Word."[3] This birthed what was called neo-Chalcedonianism. But at the Third Council of Constantinople in 680, with the definitive condemnation of the Monothelite heresy (which held that Christ had only one will, a divine will), the balance was reestablished in favor of the Chalcedonian definition.

The West did not go through the same kind of turmoil even though it actively participated in these subsequent conflicts. It had readily accepted the Chalcedonian definition and maintained it without difficulty.

THE FACE OF CHRIST IN THE EAST AND WEST

After Chalcedon, what became of the two paths or the two basic Christological models developed by Tradition? Did they disappear, leveled out by the dogmatic formulation?

On the theological level, from that time on there was certainly one faith in Christ common to East and West. Saint John of Damascus in the East and Saint Thomas Aquinas in the West both based their Christological syntheses on Chalcedon. In some ways, Saint Thomas gave new vigor to the Cyrillic insight on the unity of Christ.

If, however, we look beyond theology and dogmatics to other aspects of Church life, we see that the two Christological models or archetypes did not entirely vanish. They were preserved and left their mark: the first in Orthodox spirituality and the second in Latin spirituality. In other words, the Eastern Church favored the Johannine and Alexandrian Christ with an emphasis on the centrality of the Incarnation, the divinity of

Christ, and the concept of divinization. The Western Church favored the Pauline and Antiochene Christ with an emphasis on Christ's humanity and the paschal mystery.

Obviously this is not a rigid demarcation. Influences from each side were interwoven and varied from author to author, from era to era and from society to society. Both Churches believed, and rightly so, that they esteemed John and Paul together. Nevertheless, everyone admits that the Christ of the Byzantine tradition has different features than the Christ of the Latin tradition.

Certain details can highlight this difference. First, let us look at the *Eastern Christ*. The image in art that is most representative of Christ in the Orthodox Church is the *Pantocrator*, the glorious Christ. This is the image that the congregation sees when they look at the apse of the church. Clearly, Byzantine art is aware of the Crucified One, but he also has glorious, regal traits in which the reality of the passion is already being transformed by the light of the Resurrection. In brief, it is the Johannine Crucified One, a "glorified" Christ on the cross.

The Incarnation continues to hold first place in the mystery of Christ. Salvation is consistently conceived as a divinization of the human being through contact with the life-giving flesh of the Word. Saint Symeon the New Theologian, for example, says in one of his prayers to Christ, "By descending from your lofty sanctuary, without separating yourself from the Father's bosom, and becoming incarnate and born of the blessed Virgin Mary, you already remolded and vivified me, freed me from the guilt of my forefathers, and prepared me for the ascent to heaven."[4]

The essential thing already took place for them in the Incarnation of the Word. The idea of divinization returns to the forefront through Gregory Palamas and will characterize "Christology in late Byzantium."[5]

Does the Eastern Church then perhaps ignore the paschal mystery? On the contrary, everyone knows the extraordinary importance that the celebration of Easter has for the Orthodox. But here again there is a revealing sign: What is most valued in the paschal mystery is not so much the self-emptying but the glory, the Resurrection. In every respect their attention focuses on Christ as "God."

These characteristics are also found in the *ideal of holiness* that predominates in this spirituality. The height of holiness is considered to be the transfiguration of the saint into the image of the glorified Christ. In the lives of two of the most typical saints in orthodoxy, Saint Symeon the New Theologian and Saint Seraphim of Sarov, we find the mystical phenomenon of conformity to the radiant Christ of Tabor and of the Christ of the Resurrection. The saint appears almost transformed into light.

Let us now look at some aspects of Western spirituality. Saint Augustine writes that, of the three days "of the crucified, buried, and risen Lord" that constitute the paschal Triduum, "the cross signifies what we are doing in the present life, but what the burial and resurrection signify we have only in faith and hope."[6] In other words, while we are in this life, the crucified Christ is closer and more present to us than the risen Christ.

In fact, the typical image of Christ in Western art is the crucified Christ. The very representation of the Crucified One, at a certain point, moves away from the glorious, regal model and assumes realistic traits of true pain and even of agony. He is the Pauline Crucified One who became "sin" and "a curse" for us on the cross (see 2 Corinthians 5:21; Galatians 3:13).

Starting with Saint Bernard and then with the Franciscans, the devotion and attention to the humanity of Christ and to different "mysteries" of his life take on great importance. The *kenosis*, or self-emptying, of Christ holds first place, and with it the paschal mystery. In this context, the principle of the "imitation of Christ" established by the Antiochene school finds its practical application. It is not surprising that the most famous book of spirituality produced by the Latin Middle Ages will turn out to be precisely *The Imitation of Christ*. Contrary to any effort to bypass Christ's humanity to strive directly for union with God, Saint Teresa of Avila will affirm that there is no stage in spiritual life in which we can disregard the humanity of Christ.

The saints, here as well, furnish a kind of practical comparison. What is the sign here for the attainment of holiness? It is not conformity to the glorious Christ of the Transfiguration but conformity to the crucified Christ. The Orthodox tradition does not have examples of *stigmatized* saints although, as we saw, it does have examples of *transfigured* saints.

In some respects, the Protestant Reformation took some traits of the Western Pauline Christ and the paschal mystery to the extreme. Protestantism elevated the "theology of the cross" as the criterion for every theology, at times polemically against the "theology of glory." Søren Kierkegaard will end up asserting that we cannot know Christ in this life except in his abasement.[7]

It is true that Luther and the Protestants, in polemic against medieval excesses of the *imitation* of Christ, affirmed that Christ is above all a *gift* to be received by faith much more than he is a *model* to follow through imitation. But here again, which Christ is seen as the "gift" to receive through faith? It is not the *Logos* who descended and became flesh, but the Pauline paschal Christ,

Christ on the cross. I have already had opportunity to note how the strongest criticisms (perhaps themselves needing correction) of the Greek idea of salvation through divinization have come from Protestantism.

I repeat: There will be trouble if we make these distinctions rigid because they will become false and antihistorical. For example, in Byzantine spirituality there is a tradition of holiness called "Fools for God," in which assimilation into Christ in his *kenosis* is at the center of everything. With these qualifications, however, there remains an undeniably different emphasis already apparent in the different way of interpreting the mystery of the Transfiguration. In the West it is read in terms of the passion; in the East, in terms of Christ's divinity and glory. The West has preferred the path marked out by Paul; the East has preferred the path marked out by John. But both West and East, faithful to Chalcedon, have embraced the other pole of the mystery in their own vision, keeping the two paths connected.

The grace of the present time is that the Church, here as in other sectors of its life, is beginning to appreciate this diversity as *richness* and no longer as a *threat*. Pope John Paul II's insistence on this direction was clear, and what he wrote in *Tertio Millennio Adveniente* applies to the Orthodox Church in a very special way: "I pray that the Jubilee will be a promising opportunity for fruitful cooperation in the many areas which unite us; they are unquestionably more numerous than those which divide us."[8] In the East as well, some voices are also beginning to be heard encouraging this same direction. An orthodox theologian offered this evaluation: If the Latin understanding of Christ is taken in isolation, it can lead to a concept of the Church that is too historical, earthly and human; if the Orthodox understanding of Christ is taken by itself, it can lead to a concept of the Church that is too eschatological, disincarnated and not attentive enough to its historical duties. Because of this, he concludes, "The authentic catholicity of the church must include both East and West."[9]

In view of the new millennium, we need to present a "whole" Christ to the world, a multidimensional Christ, not a Christ who is divided up between different traditions. This does not mean we should eliminate or level out the differences that we have perceived. Once the validity and biblical character of the two different approaches are recognized, what is needed is an exchange of gifts, a respect and esteem for each other's tradition.

The doctrine of charisms needs to be applied here too: It is not necessary for every church to have the same charism, but the charism of every church should be to the benefit of all. It is as if God made two keys for us to enter into the fullness of the Christian mystery and gave one to Eastern Christianity and one to Western Christianity so that neither key can open and enter into the fullness without the other.

In Colmar, Alsace, there is a famous polyptych (a picture that is enclosed by two panels which also constitute a picture) by Matthias Grünewald. When the two panels of the polyptych are closed, we see a crucifixion, and when they are open we see the Resurrection. The crucifixion is startlingly realistic: We see an agonized Jesus with his fingers and toes contorted, jutting out like the twigs of a dry tree. The body has thorns and nails thrust into every part of it. It is the kind of painting about which Dostoevsky said, looking at it from afar, "That's a painting that might make some people lose their faith."[10] On the other hand, the Risen One in the other painting appears in such brilliant light that we can hardly see the traces of a human face. If we consider only this painting, we may not "lose our faith," but we risk losing our trust since this Christ is distant from our experience of suffering.

It leads to trouble, therefore, if we divide this polyptych or view only one part of it. It is a forceful symbol of what should happen, on a larger scale, with the Orthodox Christ and the Western Christ: They must be held together. They should not undergo the fate of some polyptychs that were disassembled over the centuries with one half ending up in one museum and the other half in another, resulting in a serious loss of our ability to understand the work of art and the intention of the artist.

BEGINNING AGAIN FROM SCRIPTURE

So far I have outlined the historical paths to approach the mystery of Christ. We cannot be content, however, to summarize and pass on only the images of Christ that have been left to us by the past, no matter how rich and profound.

We admire the paintings of Giotto and Raphael, but if one of them were to try to paint Christ today in his own style, his paintings would be considered lifeless copies and nothing more. Just as the face of Christ is renewed in art, so too—and even more so—that face needs to be renewed in our faith and in the proclamation of the gospel.

I am not here proposing a third path (which probably does not exist) but rather a new synthesis of the two traditional paths. Better yet, a new appreciation for them, a new way of presenting Jesus as a human being and Jesus as God. And this cannot happen in Christianity any other way than through beginning again from Scripture.

Reflection on Christ, under the pressure of heresies and in the encounter between the different schools, has always concentrated more on certain key texts: those on the Word becoming flesh, on Christ as the image of God, and so on. In so doing, what was built was like a cone that narrows little by little as it proceeds from the base to the top. The tip of the cone represents the Chalcedonian formula "two natures, one person."[11]

At this point two possibilities emerge. We could shape a subsequent reflection on Christ in the shape of an upside-down cone whose top lays on the tip of the preceding cone—on the formula "two natures, one person" (as the traditional treatises of Christology were conceived until the Council). On the other hand, we could start at the bottom and shape a new cone, not alongside the preceding one but encapsulating it. Plainly, in this latter case, holding very firmly to established dogma already in place, we could begin anew from all the richness of the gospel data about Christ to trace a new image, one that is living and responsive to the changing spiritual needs of the Church.

Christ for the Age of Media

I would now like to show with a concrete example what this could mean if applied to our situation today. In 1 Timothy, after exhorting Christians to pray for different categories of people, the apostle adds, "This is right and acceptable in the sight of God our Savior, who desires everyone to be saved and to come to the knowledge of the truth. For there is one God; there is also one mediator between God and humankind, Christ Jesus, himself human, who gave himself a ransom for all" (2:3–6).

In this text we find the suggestive title of *mediator*. This is the only time it explicitly appears although the concept is expressed elsewhere in other ways. The concept of mediation is central to the whole Bible and in particular to the New Testament. Two things should be noted here from the exegetical point of view. The first is the universality of Christ's mediation. The Old Testament knew Moses as the mediator between God and the people of Israel, but it was mediation in a broad sense. Moses carries out certain functions to represent the people to God and to represent God to the people, but he functions entirely from the side of human beings. There is nothing that makes him close to or equal to God. Furthermore, his mediation is localized, restricted to Israel.

This is not the case with Jesus. His mediation is *universal*, spanning both poles with God at one end and "human beings," that is, all of humanity, at the other. God, in fact, "desires everyone to be saved" (1 Timothy 2:4). Christ's mediation then is real and *personal* in the sense that he unites in his person both poles by being God and a human being. If there is an emphasis here on the qualification of being "human" (the human being Christ Jesus), it is because "it was necessary for the Son of God to become for us 'Immanuel, that is, God with us'…in such a way that his divinity and our human nature might by mutual connection grow together. Otherwise the nearness would not have been near enough."[12]

The images of Christ that we contemplated in the preceding meditations were influenced by a need for a particular kind of salvation that was felt in different milieus based on a particular conception of the human being. What aspects of salvation do people around us feel a need for today? There are many, and they cannot of course be summarized in one single word. I will try, however, to highlight one situation that is certainly characteristic of people in this new millennium.

We live in an age of mass media. The so-called "means of communication" are the great protagonists of the hour. In some societies like the one we live in, every individual can get news of what is happening in the world at any time of day or night and be in direct contact with another person any place on the planet.

All of this points to a tremendous progress for which we should be grateful to God and to the technology that has made it possible. If the Church Fathers thanked Providence for Roman roads because they helped to spread the gospel—thanks to which, they said, "we walk on the highways without fear, and sail where we will"[13]—then we should likewise be thankful for these new roads, "the information highways." Having said that, though, I would like to point out a risk in this overwhelming proliferation of communication: When it becomes an end in itself, it closes off all communication of a different nature.

What kind of communication am I talking about? A communication that I would call *self-consuming*, in the sense that it tends to exhaust itself and burn out. It is an exclusively horizontal communication. In short, it is the opposite of *creative* information, which springs up and introduces qualitatively new content, "the good news." In this self-consuming communication, human beings exchange their news and just as they are "short-lived," their news is also short-lived. One communication cancels out another, like a wave of the sea cancels the traces of the preceding wave on the shore. There is an exchange of information, of experiences, of achievements, of course, but more often than not it is an exchange about poverty, anxiety, distress, insecurity and cries for help that go unheard (not to mention the perversion that also occurs on the Internet with pedophilia).

Our experience of all this is one of being closed in, of a kind of asphyxia. Human beings have left Earth and traveled through outer space, but that has not changed anything about their existence; it has only moved the wall that encloses them by a few "centimeters." The more *communication* increases, the more the *inability to communicate* is experienced.

There have been significant literary expressions of this sense of emptiness. One is the so-called "Theater of the Absurd" where people speak and speak but do not really say anything. Communication is reduced to sounds, to noises. The noise reassures us that we are not alone. What is missing is a vertical, creative communication that really brings something new into the circle that is worth communicating. What is missing is the "totally other."

CLOSED DOORS

The best example of this state of affairs, in my opinion, is the play *No Exit* by Jean-Paul Sartre. There could not be a more striking symbol. Three people—a man and two women—are led into a room one by one during brief intervals. There are no windows, the light is very bright and cannot be turned off, the heat is suffocating, and there is nothing except a sofa for each of them. The door is of course closed; there is a doorbell, but it makes no sound. Who are these people? They are dead and have found themselves in hell. The man is a deserter who made his poor wife suffer all his life; one woman has committed infanticide and the other is a lesbian.

There are no mirrors, so they can only see themselves through the eyes and the souls of the others who reflect back the most brutal and merciless images, whose horror is deliberately increased by sarcasm. After a little while, when their souls have been laid bare to each other and the sins they are most ashamed of have risen to the surface one after another and been exposed by the others without pity, one of the characters says to the other two, "You remember all we were told about the torture-chambers, the fire and brimstone, the 'burning marl.' Old wives' tales! There's no need for red-hot pokers. Hell is—other people!"[14]

The most tragic part is that, after so much senseless verbal beating and abusing of each other, when the door unexpectedly opens—we don't know why—none of the three wants to leave anymore.

That room could be a symbol of the so-called "global village," that is, of the Earth now made small and united by modern means of communication but where human beings are truly not communicating with anyone other than themselves and, even then, at the most superficial levels. This kind of communication would turn out to be a hell because every person would become for others a mirror that reflects the image of their own misery and the echo of their own emptiness.

What could it mean, for a believer, to rediscover Jesus as the mediator between God and human beings in this context? It would mean breaking down the "closed doors," opening up a new horizon in communication, the infinite horizon of God, of mercy. Christ offers himself to us as the place of communication between God and human beings—a personal communication of truth, of meaning, of joy, of forgiveness. Mercy and forgiveness are precisely what characterize this communication. God knows our hearts and our misery, but he does not throw that in our faces; he does not reflect back to us the image that we have of ourselves and that often horrifies us, but the image he has of us. He sees us as children in the Son (see Galatians 4:5–6).

This interpretation of the "mediator" does not cancel out our status as children but is rather based on it. However, it does not stop there. Jesus is the one in whom a person can dialogue with God. "Long ago God spoke to our ancestors in many and various ways by the prophets, but in these last days he has spoken to us by a Son" (Hebrews 1:1–2). He has spoken to us, that is, not by means of someone who has interjected himself between us but personally because it says that the Son is "the reflection of God's glory and the exact imprint of God's very being" (Hebrews 1:3).

Jesus is the door through which a person can "come in and go out" (see John 10:9), the door through which a person can move about in freedom. An open door to God! "Through him both of us [Jews and gentiles] have access in one Spirit to the Father" (Ephesians 2:18). Access, portal, path—these are common terms in today's computer language. But here it is a question of access to quite different "data" and to quite different responses.

Jesus, a human being and God, could be likened to a certain house on an ordinary city street whose entrance is a door that is identical to all the others, but which, once we have entered, leads to a balcony on the opposite side which opens onto an immense mountain scene or onto the sea or onto a park full of greenery and silence. As a human being he is the open door to humanity; as God he is the balcony that opens to infinity.

The person who has come the closest to this concrete and existential understanding of "mediator" was Saint Catherine of Siena with the concept that was precious to her of Christ as a "bridge" between Earth and heaven, between God and human beings. God said to her, "The road [between God and us] was broken by...sin.... And so wishing to remedy your great evils, I have given you the Bridge of My Son."[15]

SILENCE AND PRAYER

How and where can we experience this mediator Jesus who puts us in communication with the wellspring of our being and the one who gives meaning to our lives? One helpful way is silence—creating for ourselves spaces of silence. The effect of excessive earthly and human communication is that it creates a dependency. It cannot do less; it is inevitable. What happens is what happens in Sartre's play: When the door opens, a person is no longer able to take advantage of the opportunity and leave. When the opportunity to pray is offered to us, we are no longer ready to take it. We have become resistant to deep conversation with God. Even silence itself makes us afraid.

We need to interrupt external communication every so often in order to activate interior communication, saying to ourselves with the psalmist, "Let me hear what God the LORD will speak" (Psalm 85:8). The words that Saint Anselm repeated to himself have become famous:

> Come now, insignificant man, fly for a moment from your affairs, escape for a little while from the tumult of your thoughts. Put aside now your weighty cares and leave your wearisome toils. Abandon yourself for a little to God and rest for a little in Him. Enter into

the chamber of your soul, shut out everything save God and what
can be of help in your quest for Him and having locked the door
seek Him out.[16]

It is not difficult to adapt this exhortation to our current situation: Flee for a little while the vain news of the world; turn off the radio, stop watching television, hang up the telephone, just as you do when you are about to receive an important visit and you do not want to be disturbed. You do not need to go far to find the mediator who will bring you to God. The door is always ready to open before you, as soon as you knock.

But the best path, naturally, is prayer, which silence itself should serve. The liturgy invites us to appreciate Jesus' mediation by having us pray "through him, with him, and in him." It is by prayer that we pass through the *door* who is Jesus and enter into communication with God. Jesus not only makes dialogue with God possible, he *is* our very dialogue with God. Saint Augustine says, it is Christ "who prays for us, prays in us, and is prayed to by us as our head, and he is prayed to by us as our God."[17]

To pray is "to talk with Jesus about whatever occupies our minds from morning until night." It is to recollect one's soul and, in Christ, to sink into the infinity that is God.

But there is no need for an exhortation here on prayer. It is enough that its necessity be noted in this context. Only through a renewed experience of prayer can a renewed proclamation come forth.

There is a lot of talk today about the urgency of finding suitable language to transmit the faith. According to some, this is even the number one problem in proclamation. But the more I think about this idea, the more I doubt it. Is language really the number one problem? There is a famous maxim concerning public speaking that goes back to Cato: *Rem tene, verba sequentur* ("Focus on having clearly within yourself the *thing* you want to say, and the *words* will follow"). I have experienced the truth of this maxim myself an infinite number of times. When it comes to Christian proclamation, the "thing" to grasp is not a simple subject, an idea, it is the living person of Christ.

The number one problem in the proclamation of the gospel is, then, to have Jesus Christ on the inside, to have an experience of him, to be able to say with Paul, "It is Christ who lives in me" (Galatians 2:20). The proclamation is alive if Christ is alive in the person who proclaims him. Otherwise, there is no language that can solve our problems. Christian preaching, it has been rightly said, is not just the communication of ideas but, first and foremost, the communication of life.

The importance of the contemplation of Christ, which has been the focus of our approach to the mystery of the Transfiguration, is based on this. Many wealthy people in wealthy nations have two homes today: one in the city and one in the mountains. The mountain home becomes a refuge for weekends, for vacations, whenever people can leave life's treadmill and find some time of tranquility. Let us also make for ourselves a home in the mountains! On Mount Tabor! Let us seek refuge there in spirit, every time that our duties allow, to contemplate the radiant face of Christ and imprint it on our hearts in such a way that when we need to talk about him, we would do so, as the ancient constitution of my Capuchin order says, "with an overflowing of affection."

Coming down from there, we will be able to say what Saint Peter says in his second letter, recalling the Transfiguration: "For we did not follow cleverly devised myths when we made known to you the power and coming of our Lord Jesus Christ, but we had been eyewitnesses of his majesty...while we were with him on the holy mountain" (2 Peter 1:16, 18).

NOTES

CHAPTER I

EYEWITNESSES OF HIS MAJESTY
A Mystagogical Approach to the Transfiguration

1. Pope Leo the Great, "Sermon 51," 3, in *St. Leo the Great: Sermons*, trans. Jane P. Freeland and Agnes J. Conway, vol. 93, *The Fathers of the Church* (Washington, D.C.: Catholic University of America Press, 1996), p. 220.

2. Thomas Aquinas, "Of Christ's Transfiguration," III, q. 45, a. 1, *Summa Theologica*, vol. 4, trans. Fathers of the English Dominican Province (Westminster, Md.: Christian Classics, 1981), p. 2255.

3. Anastasius of Sinai, "Homily for the Feast of the Holy Transfiguration," in Michel Coune, *Joie de la transfiguration d'après les Pères d'Orient* [The joy of the Transfiguration in the Eastern fathers] (Bellefontaine: Abbaye de Bellefontaine, 1985), vol. 39, *Spiritualité orientale* [Eastern spirituality], pp. 153–154.

4. Pope Leo the Great, "Sermon 51," 3, p. 220.

5. Pope Leo the Great, "Sermon 51," 4, p. 221.

6. "The Council of Chalcedon," in Josef Neuner and Jacques Dupuis, *The Christian Faith in the Doctrinal Documents of the Catholic Church*, ed. Jacques Dupuis (New York: Alba House, 2000), p. 227.

7. Gerhard von Rad, *Old Testament Theology, Vol. II: The Theology of Israel's Prophetic Traditions*, trans. D.M.G. Stalker (New York: Harper and Row, 1965), p. 96.

8. Augustine, "Letter 55," 2, in *Letters 1–99*, trans. Roland Teske, Part II, vol. 1 of *The Works of Saint Augustine*, ed. John E. Rotelle (Hyde Park, N.Y.: New City, 2001), p. 216.

9. Proclus of Constantinople, "First Homily on the Transfiguration," in Coune, p. 79.

10. Pope Leo the Great, "Sermon 51," 3, p. 220.

11. Anastasius of Sinai, in Coune, p. 163.

12. See Hermann Josef Sieben, "Transfiguration," in *Dictionnaire de spiritualité ascétique et mystique, doctrine et histoire* [Dictionary of ascetic and mystical spirituality, doctrine and history], vol. 15, ed. Marcel Viller and others (Paris: Beauchesne, 1990), col. 1159–1160.

13. *The Jerusalem Bible* (Garden City, N.Y.: Doubleday, 1966), 2 Cor 3:18, note e, p. 313.

14. Philotheos of Sinai, *Forty Texts on Watchfulness*, 23, vol. 3, *The Philokalia*, trans. G.E.H. Palmer and others (Boston: Faber and Faber, 1984), p. 25.

15. Pope Paul VI, *Meditazioni inedite* [Unpublished meditations] (Brescia: Istitutio Paolo VI, 1993), p. 76.

16. C.H. Dodd, *History and the Gospel* (London: Hodder and Houghton, 1938), p. 20.

17. Heinz Schürmann, *Il Vangelo di Luca* [The Gospel of Luke], vol. 1 (Brescia: Morcelliana, 1983), p. 883.

18. See Paul Evdokimov, *Saint Seraphim of Sarov: An Icon of Orthodox Spirituality* (Minneapolis: Light and Life, 1988), p. 18.

19. Origen, *Commentary on Matthew*, XII, 38, trans. John Patrick, vol. 9, *The Ante-Nicene Fathers*, ed. Allan Menzies (New York: Charles Scribner's Sons, 1926), p. 470.

CHAPTER 2
TRANSFIGURED BEFORE THEM
On Tabor With the Three Apostles

1. John of the Cross, *The Ascent of Mount Carmel,* I, 1, stanza 1, trans. and ed. E. Allison Peers (Liguori, Mo.: Triumph, 1991), p. 17.

2. The translation for Psalm 57:7 here is from *Christian Prayer: The Liturgy of the Hours* (Boston: Daughters of St. Paul, 1976), p. 620, in order to follow Fr. Cantalamessa's original more clearly.

3. John Chrysostom, *Eclogues*, 21, 12 (PG 63), p. 700.

4. John of Damascus, "Homily for the Feast of the Transfiguration," in Coune, p. 199.

5. John II of Jerusalem, "Homily for the Feast of the Transfiguration," in Coune, p. 69.

6. See Anastasius of Sinai, in Coune, pp. 158 ff.

7. Francis of Assisi, "A Letter to the Entire Order," 25, in *Francis and Clare: The Complete Works*, intro. and trans. Regis J. Armstrong and Ignatius C. Brady (New York: Paulist, 1982), pp. 57–58.

8. Gerhard von Rad, *Old Testament Theology, Vol. I: The Theology of Israel's Historical Traditions*, trans. D.M.G. Stalker (New York: Harper and Row, 1962), p. 365.

9. Von Rad, vol. 1, p. 366.

10. Anastasius of Sinai, in Coune, p. 154; see Paul Evdokimov, *The Art of the Icon: The Theology of Beauty*, trans. Steven Bigham (Redondo Beach, Calif.: Oakwood, 1990).

11. Plato, *The Republic*, trans. Richard W. Sterling and William C. Scott (New York: Norton, 1996), p. 198.

12. Augustine, *Confessions*, X, 27, trans. Maria Boulding, vol. 1, *The Works of Saint Augustine*, ed. John E. Rotelle (Hyde Park, N.Y.: New City, 1997), p. 262.

13. Augustine, *Confessions*, X, 34, p. 272.

14. Fyodor Dostoevsky, letter to his niece Sonja Ivanova, January 13, 1868, trans. David A. Love in *Dostoevsky's "The Idiot": A Critical Companion*, ed. Liza Knapp (Evanston, Ill.: Northwestern University Press, 1998), pp. 242–243.

15. Augustine, "Sermon 78," 3, trans. Edmund Hill, vol. 3, *The Works of Saint Augustine*, ed. John E. Rotelle (New York: New City, 1991), p. 341.

16. Augustine, "Sermon 78," 6, pp. 342–343.

17. Raymond of Capua, *The Life of St. Catherine of Siena*, trans. George Lamb (New York: P.J. Kennedy and Sons, 1960), p. 43.

18. Raymond of Capua, p. 43.

19. Schürmann, p. 874.

20. See Origen, *Commentary on Matthew*, XII, 42, pp. 472–473.

21. Augustine, "Sermon 79," 1, p. 345.

22. John of the Cross, *The Ascent of Mount Carmel*, II, 22, 5, p. 164.

23. See Diadochos of Photiki, *On Spiritual Knowledge and Discernment: 100 Texts*, 39, vol. 1, *The Philokalia*, trans. G.E.H. Palmer and others (Boston: Faber and Faber, 1979), p. 265.

24. Origen, *Commentary on Matthew*, XII, 43, p. 473.

CHAPTER 3

I Want to Know Christ
On Tabor With Paul

1. *Ipsius sunt tempora et saecula.* See the prayer "Blessing of the Fire and the Lighting of the Candle" for the Easter Vigil.

2. For example, see Cyril of Alexandria, "Letter 55," 23: "The Word became man without ceasing to be what he was," *St. Cyril of Alexandria: Letters 51–110*, trans. John I. McEnerny, vol. 77, *The Fathers of the Church* (Washington, D.C.: Catholic University of America Press, 1985), p. 24.

3. Irenaeus, *Against Heresies*, IV, 10, 1 and IV; 26, 1, vol. 1, *The Ante-Nicene Fathers,* ed. Alexander Roberts and James Donaldson (New York: Charles Scribner's Sons, 1926), pp. 473, 496.

4. See Oscar Cullman, *Christ and Time*, third ed. (Oxford: Clarendon, 1962).

5. See Søren Kierkegaard, *Concluding Unscientific Postscript to Philosophical Fragments*, in *The Essential Kierkegaard*, ed. Howard V. and Edna H. Hong (Princeton, N.J.: Princeton University Press, 1995), pp. 210–212.

6. See *Didache, The Apostolic Fathers,* trans. J.B. Lightfoot and J.R. Harmer, second ed. (Grand Rapids: Baker, 1989), pp. 153–155.

7. Tertullian, *Against Praxeas,* 27, in *The Christological Controversy*, trans. and ed. Richard A. Norris, Jr. (Philadelphia: Fortress, 1980), p. 63.

8. Thomas of Celano, *The First Life of St. Francis*, 103, in *Saint Francis of Assisi*, trans. Placid Hermann (Chicago: Franciscan Herald, 1963), p. 94.

CHAPTER 4

In the Beginning Was the Word
On Tabor With John

1. Aurelius Symmachus, *Prefect and Emperor: The "Relationes" of Symmachus, A.D. 364*, trans. R.H. Barrow (Oxford: Clarendon, 1973), p. 41. "*Uno itinere non potest perveniri ad tam grande secretum.*"

2. C.H. Dodd, *The Interpretation of the Fourth Gospel* (Cambridge: Cambridge University Press, 1953), p. 268.

3. Augustine, *The City of God*, X, 29, trans. John Healey (New York: Dutton, 1948), p. 305.

4. "An Ancient Christian Sermon" ["2 Clement"], 9, 5, in *The Apostolic Fathers*, trans. J.B. Lightfoot and J.R. Harmer, second ed. (Grand Rapids: Baker, 1989), p. 72.

5. Célestin Charlier, *Giovanni l'Evangelista: Meditazione Liturgica del Prologo* [John the Evangelist: Liturgical Meditations on the Prologue] (Rome: Edizioni Paoline, 1981), p. 115.

6. *Gaudium et Spes*, Pastoral Constitution on the Church in the Modern World, 38, in *The Documents of Vatican II*, ed. Walter M. Abbott (New York: Guild, 1966), p. 236.

7. "Epistle to Diognetus," 5, 1ff., in *The Apostolic Fathers*, p. 299.

8. T.S. Eliot, *The Family Reunion*, Act II, scene 2, in *The Complete Plays and Poems* (New York: Harcourt, Brace and World, 1971), p. 281.

9. Jacques Guillet, "Jésus," in *Dictionnaire de spiritualité ascétique et mystique, doctrine et histoire* [Dictionary of ascetic and mystical spirituality, doctrine and history], vol. 8, ed. Marcel Viller and others (Paris: Beauchesne, 1974), col. 1098.

10. See Origen, *Contra Celsum*, VI, 10, trans. Frederick Crombie, vol. 4, *The Ante-Nicene Fathers*, ed. Alexander Roberts and James Donaldson (Grand Rapids: Eerdmans, 1956), p. 577; cf. II, 31, p. 444.

11. See Origen, I, 26–28, pp. 407–408.

12. "Severus Alexander," 43, 6, *The Scriptores Historiae Augustae*, trans. David Magie (New York: Putnam's Sons, 1924), p. 267.

13. Origen, *Commentary on John*, I, 23, trans. Ronald Heine, vol. 80, *The Fathers of the Church* (Washington, D.C.: Catholic University of America Press, 1989), p. 38.

CHAPTER 5

THE WORD BECAME FLESH
A Contemplation of Christ in His Divinity

1. Athanasius, *Against the Arians*, II, 8, trans. Alexander Robertson, vol. 4, *Nicene and Post-Nicene Fathers of the Christian Church*, ed. Philip Schaff and Henry Wace (Grand Rapids: Eerdmans, 1956), p. 352.

2. Athanasius, *The Incarnation of the Word of God*, 17, trans. a religious of C.S.M.V. S.Th. (New York: Macmillan, 1946), p. 45.

3. Athanasius, *The Incarnation of the Word of God*, 8, p. 34; see *Against the Arians*, III, 35, p. 413.

4. See Athanasius, *Against the Arians*, III, 43 and 54, p. 417, p. 423.

5. See Athanasius, *Against the Arians*, III, 42–43, pp. 416–417.

6. Cyril of Alexandria, *On the Unity of Christ*, trans. and intro. John Anthony McGuckin (Crestwood, N.Y.: St. Vladimir's Seminary Press, 1995), p. 54; see *Against Nestorius*, V, 2, pp. 161ff.

7. See Cyril of Alexandria, p. 122.

8. Cyril's famous phrase as quoted in John Anthony McGuckin's introduction in *On the Unity of Christ*, p. 45; see also "The Second Council of Constantinople" in Josef Neuner and Jacques Dupuis, *The Christian Faith in the Doctrinal Documents of the Catholic Church*, ed. Jacques Dupuis, seventh ed. rev. (New York: Alba House, 2001), p. 234.

9. See the text in *Enchiridion Oecumenicum*, 3 (Bologna: Dehoniane, 1995), pp. 1113ff.

10. "The union between full divinity and humanity in the one (divine) person of Jesus Christ," which occurred at the Incarnation. See Gerald O'Collins and Edward G. Farrugia, *A Concise Dictionary of Theology* (New York: Paulist, 1991), p. 98.

11. See Cyril of Alexandria, "Third Letter to Nestorius" (Epistle 17), in *Christianity in Late Antiquity, 300–450 C.E.: A Reader*, ed. Bart D. Ehrman and Andrew S. Jacobs (New York: Oxford University Press, 2004), pp. 183–188.

12. Pope John Paul II, *Redemptoris Missio*, Mission of the Redeemer, 6 (Boston: Daughters of St. Paul, 1990), p. 15.

13. See Athanasius, *The Incarnation of the Word of God*, 54, p. 93.

14. See Athanasius, *The Incarnation of the Word of God*, 8, p. 34; see *Against the Arians*, III, 33, pp. 411–412.

15. See Gregory of Nazianzus, "Third Theological Oration," 19, in *Christianity in Late Antiquity*, p. 175.

16. Athanasius, *Against the Arians*, II, 59, p. 380; see "Epistle 1," 23, in *The Armenian Version of the Letters of Athanasius to Bishop Serapion*

Concerning the Holy Spirit, ed. Jacob Geerlings, trans. George A. Egan (Salt Lake City: University of Utah Press, 1968), pp. 159–160.

17. See Athanasius, *The Incarnation of the Word of God*, 20, p. 49; see pp. 190–200.

18. Athanasius, *The Incarnation of the Word of God*, 20, p. 49.

19. Cyril of Alexandria, *Easter Homilies* 17, 4, *Patrologia Graeca*, 77, pp. 785ff.

20. Cyril of Alexandria, *Easter Homilies* 10, 2, *Patrologia Graeca*, 77, p. 617D.

21. "The self-communication of God (often called *uncreated grace*) means the deification of human life (2 Peter 1:4) and lifts to a new and undeserved level the relationship of creature to creator" (O'Collins and Farrugia, p. 86).

22. Cyril of Alexandria, *Commentary on John*, IV, 2, trans. and intro. Norman Russell (New York: Routledge, 2000), p. 117.

23. Cyril of Alexandria, *Commentary on John*, IV, 2, pp. 117–118.

24. Cyril of Alexandria, *Commentary on John*, IV, 2, p. 119.

25. Cyril of Alexandria, *Commentary on John*, IV, 2, p. 118.

26. Cyril of Alexandria, *Glaphyra in Genesim*, 1, 5, *Patrologia Graeca*, 69, p. 29B.

27. Cyril of Alexandria, *Commentary on John*, IV, 3, pp. 119ff.

28. Cyril of Alexandria, *Commentary on John*, IV, 2, p. 119.

29. *Communicatio idiomatum*: "the exchange of attributes because of the union of divinity and humanity in the one person of the incarnate Son of God… , e.g., 'The Son of God died on the cross,' and 'The Son of Mary created the world'" (see O'Collins and Farrugia, p. 41).

30. Nicholas Cabasilas, *The Life in Christ*, IV, 6, trans. Carmino J. deCatanzaro (Crestwood N.Y.: St. Vladimir's Seminary Press, 1974), p. 122.

31. Cabasilas, IV, 6, p. 123.

32. Cabasilas, IV, 8, p. 125.

33. Gregory Palamas, *Triads in Defense of the Holy Hesychasts*, I, 3, quoted in John Meyendorff, *Christ in Eastern Christian Thought* (Crestwood, N.Y.: St. Vladimir's Seminary Press, 1987), p. 206.

CHAPTER 6

OBEDIENT UNTO DEATH
A Contemplation of Christ in His Humanity

1. Theodore of Mopsuestia, *Catechesis*, VI, 5 [Theodore on the Nicene Creed], ed. and trans. Alphonse Mingana, vol. 5, *Woodbrooke Studies* (Cambridge: Heffer and Sons, 1932), p. 65.

2. See Theodore of Mopsuestia, *Catechesis*, VIII, 1, 13, 16, pp. 82ff.; see Nestorius, "Letter to Cyril of Alexandria," in *Christianity in Late Antiquity*, pp. 180–182.

3. Theodore of Mopsuestia, *Catechesis*, VI, 8, p. 67.

4. Theodore of Mopsuestia, *Catechesis*, VI, 10, p. 69.

5. See Richard A. Norris, Jr., *Manhood in Christ: A Study in the Christology of Theodore of Mopsuestia* (Oxford: Clarendon, 1963), p. 224.

6. Theodore of Mopsuestia, *Catechesis*, VIII, 3, p. 84.

7. Theodore of Mopsuestia, *Fragmenta Syriaca*, in Norris, *Manhood in Christ*, p. 204.

8. See Cyril of Alexandria, "Letter to Anastasius et al." (Letter 55), trans. John I. McEnerney, vol. 77, *The Fathers of the Church* (Washington, D.C.: Catholic University of America Press, 1985), pp. 30–31.

9. Narsai (d. 502), "Homily XVII: An Exposition of the Mysteries," ed. J. Armitage Robinson, vol. 8, *Texts and Studies: Contributions to Biblical and Patristic Literature* (Cambridge: Cambridge University Press, 1916; reprint, Wiesbaden: Lessing-Druckerei, 1967), pp. 14–15.

10. Theodore of Mopsuestia, *Catechesis*, VIII, 13, p. 89.

11. Theodore of Mopsuestia, Fragment of *On the Incarnation*, 8, in *The Christological Controversy*, trans. and ed. Richard A. Norris, Jr. (Philadelphia: Fortress, 1980), p. 120.

12. See O'Collins and Farrugia, p. 41.

13. See Theodore of Mopsuestia, *Catechesis*, IV, 4, p. 45.

14. Theodore of Mopsuestia, "Exegetical Fragments," in Norris, *Manhood in Christ*, p. 140.

15. Theodore of Mopsuestia, *Commentary on Romans*, XI, 15, in Norris, *Manhood in Christ*, p. 130.

16. Theodore of Mopsuestia, *Catechesis*, V, 12, 14, pp. 57–58.

17. Gregory of Nazianzus, "Epistle 101," in *The Later Christian Fathers*, ed. and trans. Henry Betterson (New York: Oxford University Press, 1970), p. 108.

18. Nestorius, *The Bazaar of Heracleides*, I, 1, 68–69, intro. and trans. G.R. Driver and Leonard Hodgson (Oxford: Clarendon, 1925), p. 63.

19. Theodore of Mopsuestia, *Catechesis*, VII, 4, p. 75.

20. Theodore of Mopsuestia, *Catechesis*, VIII, 9, p. 87.

21. See Maximus the Confessor, "Opuscule 7" ("Letter to Marinus"), in *Maximus the Confessor*, intro. and trans. Andrew Louth (New York: Routledge, 1996), pp. 180–191.

22. Theodore of Mopsuestia, *Catechesis*, XV, 15 [Theodore on the Lord's Prayer and Sacraments], ed. and trans. Alphonse Mingana, vol. 6, *Woodbrooke Studies* (Cambridge: Heffer and Sons, 1933), p. 79.

23. Theodore of Mopsuestia, *Catechesis*, XVI, 12, vol. 6, p. 104.

24. Theodore of Mopsuestia, *Catechesis*, XVI, 26, vol. 6, p. 112.

25. Theodore of Mopsuestia, *Catechesis*, VI, 11, vol. 5, p. 69.

26. Søren Kierkegaard, *The Sickness Unto Death* in *The Essential Kierkegaard*, p. 371.

27. Kierkegaard, *The Sickness Unto Death*, p. 367.

28. Theodore of Mopsuestia, *Catechesis*, VI, 4, vol. 5, p. 64.

29. *Enhypostasia*: "The doctrine of Christ's full human nature... being assumed by the person of the Logos" (O'Collins and Farrugia, p. 65).

30. Piet Schoonenberg, *The Christ: A Study of the God-Man Relationship*, trans. Della Couling (New York: Herder and Herder, 1971), p. 87.

31. See Luigi Scipioni, *Nestorio e il Concilio di Efeso* [Nestorius and the Council of Ephesus] (Milan: Vita e pensiero, 1974), pp. 365ff.

CHAPTER 7
THE MEDIATOR
An Image of Christ for the Third Millennium

1. "The Council of Chalcedon," in Josef Neuner, S.J., and Jacques Dupuis, S.J., *The Christian Faith in the Doctrinal Documents of the Catholic Church*, ed. Jacques Dupuis, seventh ed. rev. (New York: Alba House, 2001), p. 228.

2. "The Council of Chalcedon," in Neuner and Dupuis, p. 228.

3. "The Second Council of Constantinople," in Neuner and Dupuis, p. 234.

4. Symeon the New Theologian, *Hymns and Prayers*, in *Sources Chrétiennes*, 196, p. 332; see also Symeon the New Theologian, *Hymns of Divine Love*, intro. and trans. George A. Maloney (Denville, N.J.: Dimension, 1976).

5. See the title for chapter ten in John Meyendorff, *Christ in the Eastern Christian Thought*, pp. 193–207.

6. Augustine, "Letter 55," 14, trans. Roland Teske, Part II, vol. 1 of *The Works of Saint Augustine*, p. 227.

7. Søren Kierkegaard, *Practice in Christianity*, in *The Essential Kierkegaard*, pp. 381ff.

8. Pope John Paul II, *Tertio Millennio Adveniente* [As the third millennium of the new age draws near], 16 (Vatican City: Libreria Editrice Vaticana, 1974), p. 21.

9. Petros B. Vasiliadis, in *Vedere Dio* [To see God] (Bologna: Dehoniane, 1994), p. 97.

10. Fyodor Dostoevsky, *The Idiot*, II, 4, trans. Henry and Olga Carlisle (New York: New English Library, 1969), p. 238.

11. "The Council of Chalcedon," in Neuner and Dupuis, p. 228.

12. John Calvin, *Institutes of the Christian Religion*, II, 12, 1, trans. Ford Lewis Battles, vol. 20, *The Library of Christian Classics*, ed. John T. McNeill (Philadelphia: Westminster, 1960), p. 464.

13. Irenaeus, *Against Heresies*, IV, 30, 3, *The Ante-Nicene Fathers*, vol. 1, p. 503.

14. Jean-Paul Sartre, *No Exit* [*Huis clos*], scene 5, in *"No Exit" and Three Other Plays* (New York: Vintage, 1955), p. 47.

15. Catherine of Siena, *The Dialogue of the Seraphic Virgin Catherine of Siena*, trans. Algar Thorold (Westminster, Md.: Newman, 1950), p. 74.

16. Anselm, *Proslogion*, I, intro. and trans. M.J. Charlesworth (Notre Dame, Ind.: University of Notre Dame Press, 1979), p. 111.

17. Augustine, "Exposition of Psalm 85," 1, *Exposition of the Psalms 73–98*, trans. Maria Boulding, vol. 18 of *The Works of Saint Augustine*, ed. John E. Rotelle (Hyde Park, N.Y.: New City, 2002), p. 220.

Also from Raniero Cantalamessa

SOBER INTOXICATION OF THE SPIRIT
Filled with the Fullness of God
Father Raniero Cantalamessa, O.F.M. CAP.
Translated by Marsha Daigle-Williamson, PH.D.

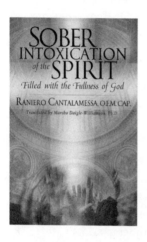

We tend to overlook Peter's opening words to the crowd that first Pentecost morning, to our own peril. His denial of drunkenness in the wake of the outpouring of the Holy Spirit should stop us in our tracks. What was going on here? How did the apostles experience the Holy Spirit? What was he teaching them? How was he empowering them? What does this scene in the streets of Jerusalem mean for us today?

Raniero Cantalamessa offers pastoral advice and leads the reader through passages of Scripture and the Fathers of the Church to remind us of the incalculable power of the Spirit available to us. This spiritual "intoxication" is an infilling—through the sacraments, especially the Eucharist, and the action of God—that purifies us of sin, renews the heart and enlightens the mind. As St. Augustine said of the Spirit, "He found you empty and he filled you…I like this kind of intoxication. The Spirit of God is both drink and light."

ISBN 978-0-86716-713-9
Price: $12.99

LOVING THE CHURCH
Scriptural Meditations for the Papal Household
Raniero Cantalamessa, O.F.M. CAP.
Translated by Gilberto Cavazos-González, O.F.M., and Amanda Quantz

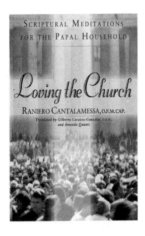

In these reflections on the Letter to the Ephesians, Father Cantalamessa, preacher to the papal household, asks a critical question: How can we read, "'And Christ loved the Church' [Eph. 5:25], without asking the question, 'And I? Do I love the Church?'" The twentieth century was a time of theological ferment focusing attention on the nature of the Church. But, the author wonders, "Was there a proportionate growth in love for the Church?"

Do we love the Church? Do we understand its nature? Do we weep over its sins or merely criticize? Are we building up or tearing down? Father Cantalamessa explores the Church as building, body, bride and mother—and also examines the family, the domestic church—in this inspirational meditation on the meaning of Church for each of us.

ISBN 978-0-86716-637-8
Price: $9.99